history
maker

DESTINY IMAGE BOOKS

by Dr. Cindy Trimm

The 40 Day Soul Fast

40 Days to Discovering the Real You

Reclaim Your Soul

40 Days to Reclaiming Your Soul

The Prosperous Soul

40 Days to a Prosperous Soul

PUSH

PREVAIL

history maker

ARISE AND TAKE YOUR PLACE IN LEADING CHANGE

Dr. Cindy Trimm

DESTINY IMAGE® PUBLISHERS, INC.
P.O. Box 310, Shippensburg, PA 17257-0310
"Promoting Inspired Lives"

This book and all other Destiny Image and Destiny Image Fiction books are available at Christian bookstores and distributors worldwide.   .

For more information on foreign distributors, call 717-532-3040.
Reach us on the Internet: www.destinyimage.com.

Cover design by Prodigy Pixel
Manuscript prepared by Rick Killian, Killian Creative, Boulder, Colorado.
www.killiancreative.com
Interior design by Susan Ramundo

ISBN 13 TP: 978-0-7684-1708-1
ISBN 13 Ebook: 978-0-7684-1709-8
ISBN 13 HC: 978-0-7684-1710-4
ISBN 13 LP: 978-0-7684-1711-1

For Worldwide Distribution, Printed in the U.S.A.
1 2 3 4 5 6 7 8 / 21 20 19 18 17

*To all of the "unknown heroes" who are working
in communities around the world in quiet, unseen ways,
bringing hope and healing wherever they are.
You are the true history makers and
unsung champions of change.*

*This book is dedicated to honoring the capacity of the
human spirit and the potential hidden within every soul...*

*"That no good cause shall lack a champion, and that
evil shall not thrive unopposed."*

—Carlton Benjamin Goodlett

The moment we recognize that we are empowered beings called to live life on purpose with hope and dignity, we can all rise up. We can call forth the hidden potential and greatness within us, and be the change the world so desperately needs.

Praise for *History Maker*

Dr. Cindy Trimm is a profound and prolific communicator of truth.

T.D. Jakes
New York Times bestselling author

[*History Maker* is] the perfect message for our time. If you want to change the world, start by getting aligned with your soul's purpose. This book provides the stories that will inspire you on this journey.

Richard Barrett
Founder and Chairman of the Barrett Values Centre
Author of *Love, Fear, and the Destiny of Nations*

Dr. Cindy Trimm is a pioneer and prolific voice for this generation. In this book, *History Maker*, she does an amazing job of challenging us to see the history maker in ourselves and allowing that person to grow into their fullest potential. *History Maker* is important for this generation because, in order for us to radically alter our futures, the person within has to be energized and inspired; this book does just that! It speaks to the ordinary person and informs them of the more that is within them. I highly recommend this book!

Dr. Matthew Stevenson
Author and Senior Pastor of All Nations Worship Assembly
Overseer of the GATE Network of Churches

With poise and logic, Dr. Trimm's *History Maker* spiritually challenges us to rationally recognize and revolutionize our thought processes by unleashing our inner power as we move to transform the future of new thinkers and leaders! *History Maker* is an indispensable guide to releasing our inner strength while influencing, inspiring, and empowering generations to come.

DeVon Franklin
President and CEO of Franklin Entertainment, member of the
Academy of Motion Picture Arts and Sciences, award-winning film and TV
producer, New York Times best-selling author,
former Senior Vice President of Columbia Pictures

Once again Cindy Trimm delivers a book rich in wisdom, practical application, deep biblical truths, and leadership principles we all can embrace in our quest to becoming *History Makers*.

Lori George Billingsley
Public Relations Executive

Great leaders will need to prepare for a future world of disruptions, decentralization, volatility, complexity, and ambiguity. *History Maker* is a visionary book that provides deep insight into leadership concepts for those seeking a fresh viewpoint and a new way forward.

Sarah-Elizabeth Reed
Board of Regents, University Systems of Georgia
and wife of Atlanta Mayor Kasim Reed

History Maker is an insightful, practical, faith-based response for people seeking to make a positive difference in their own life and the lives of others. As we attempt to navigate the enormous challenges and changes taking place in humanity, this book blends ancient wisdom together with modern stories and observations to deepen the dialogue and help us find our individual and collective paths.

Phil Clothier
CEO of the Barrett Values Centre

History Maker is a marvelous extension of the work I've witnessed Dr. Cindy Trimm practice through the Adopt-A-City program that she established in the McFarland, California community. The book is a must-read for social innovators, political and business leaders, and for every curious reader seeking to move beyond theory to practicing positive social change and reconstruction throughout their organizations, communities, and nations.

The Honorable Manuel Cantu
Mayor of McFarland, California

Through her new book, *History Maker*, Dr. Cindy Trimm provides a proven blueprint to discovering all God has deposited into your life so you can walk boldly in your ordained state of greatness. Dr. Trimm has no rival when it comes to advanced life strategies. Read her wisdom, study it, meditate on it, and apply its principles to position yourself among the history makers.

Kevin Mullens
Author, Executive Movie Producer, Global Business Builder

Once again, Dr. Trimm has delivered a timeless, cutting-edge message that will shift culture forward and inspire us towards personal wholeness and professional breakthrough. Dr. Trimm is one of the foremost thought leaders of this generation and through harnessing her profound knowledge of faith, business, philosophy and politics, is empowering a movement of history-making women.

Jessica Littles
Contributor, *Essence Magazine*

You will be inspired, encouraged, empowered, informed, and excited about your future. Dr. Cindy Trimm has made the commitment to help people globally realize that although they may not have started life with much, they can finish with much.

Dr. Willie Jolley
Bestselling Author, Speaker

Dr. Cindy Trimm is recognized around the world as a renowned author, dynamic speaker, global strategist, and a trusted voice of hope.

Bishop Paul S. Morton
Senior pastor, Changing a Generation FGBC, Atlanta, GA

Dr. Trimm offers practical advice for moving beyond the bounds of "ordinary" to achieve the vibrancy and vitality of life lived anticipating the extraordinary.

Dr. Rod Parsley
Pastor, World Harvest Church,
Columbus, Ohio

Let no one be discouraged by the belief there is nothing one person can do against the enormous array of the world's ills, misery, ignorance, and violence. Few will have the greatness to bend history itself, but each of us can work to change a small portion of events. It is from numberless diverse acts of courage and belief that human history is shaped.

Each time a man stands up for an ideal, or acts to improve the lot of others, or strikes out against injustice, he sends forth a tiny ripple of hope, and crossing each other from a million different centers of energy and daring, those ripples build a current which can sweep down the mightiest walls of oppression and resistance.

—ROBERT F. KENNEDY, "DAY OF AFFIRMATION"

contents

Part Three: Shaping History

Don't stand idly by when your neighbor's life is at stake.

—Leviticus 19:16 CJB

The opposite of love is not hate; it's indifference.
The opposite of beauty is not ugliness; it's indifference.
The opposite of faith is not heresy; it's indifference.
Indifference, to me, is the epitome of evil.

—Elie Wiesel

Morally speaking, there is no limit to the concern one must feel for the suffering of human beings, that indifference to evil is worse than evil itself; in a free society, some are guilty, but all are responsible.

—Abraham Joshua Heschel

Let there be peace on earth, and let it begin with me.

—Sy Miller and Jill Jackson

foreword

As the daughter of parents that were "world changers" and who grasped the importance of changing one's self as a prerequisite to changing the world—I believe that *History Maker* continues my father's message into the 21st century.

In the Movement led by my father, Martin Luther King, Jr., he embodied and injected a nonviolent philosophy that worked on healing one's interior self before attempting to heal the ills of society. Through this philosophy, my father and others in the Movement were able to change the south, the nation, and as a result, the entire world.

Changing the world begins with each of us allowing our souls to be healed and made whole again. The more we do this inner work of healing—what in many ways is spiritual healing—the more the world around us will be healed and made whole. The world we experience, after all, is nothing more than the sum of the individuals who inhabit it. It is only a reflection of what we harbor in our hearts—whether fear, prejudice, greed, or love.

History Maker is a guide to aid each of us in our common quest to transform our world and to ultimately establish what my father called the Beloved Community, which is at the heart of the Kingdom of God.

As the keeper of my parents' legacy, I take very seriously the words that I use to compare the work of others to the works and message of my parents. This endorsement I believe speaks volumes regarding what I believe about Dr. Trimm as a global leader and the potential impact of her message and the work she tirelessly pursues around the world.

It is my belief that *History Maker* will enhance every reader's leadership capabilities and therefore their capacity to impact not only their own career and professional field, but also the culture in which they are seeded and the continents upon which they live. I believe that Dr. Trimm is the voice of hope we so desperately need to hear in this season.

I know Dr. Cindy Trimm both professionally and personally and applaud the good work she continues to do around the world as a distinguished advisor, life strategist, bestselling author, and global leader. Thank you, Dr. Trimm, for so faithfully carrying forward the history-making legacy my parents so passionately gave their lives for.

—Bernice King, Author of *Hard Questions Heart Answers*

Rarely do I come across a writer whose work I feel is at the cutting edge of the evolution of human consciousness. When I read *History Maker,* I knew I had come across such a person. I knew immediately that Cindy's and my souls had come out of the same mold. Cindy knows she doesn't have an inner core, a higher self, or a soul: she knows she *is* her inner core; she *is* her higher self; and she *is* her soul. As such, she knows she has a direct connection to God.

Over the past few years, I have asked thousands of people all over the world, "Do you *have* a soul or *are* you a soul." They normally answer "Yes" to both questions. Why? Because they are confused. They don't know if they are a body with a soul, or a soul with a body.

Cindy knows she is a soul with a body—and it is this understanding that makes her writing so inspirational. When you fully accept who you are, it changes your life completely; night changes to day, sadness changes to joy, and depression and brokenness change to wellbeing and wholeness. Once you understand who you are, you can become a history maker because you know your life is divinely guided. All you have to do is get out of the way.

What does it mean to "get out of the way?" First and foremost, it means releasing the fears of your ego about getting your survival, safety, and security needs met—and secondly, it means surrendering your decision-making to your soul. If you think you need something outside of yourself to be happy, you are living in ego consciousness.

When you let go of the illusion that you lack something and surrender your life to your soul, you will find that all of your needs are met before you even know you have them. If you can trust your soul to guide your life, you will be living the life you were meant to live. You will become among the few who make history, simply by honouring the sacred potential seeded within your soul. And as a result, your life will be increasingly filled with joy and meaning.

A soul is birthed into the earth for three reasons: 1) to fully express itself so it can uniquely reflect its Creator; 2) to connect with others to help them better know and reflect their own inherent divinity; and 3) within the context of divine community, to advance and prosper the human experience—and thereby shape history.

When you realize we are all souls having a human experience, and that at a higher level of consciousness we are individuated aspects of the same divine energy, the act of giving becomes the same as receiving. In other words, when I give to you, I am giving to another aspect of myself. Also, when I forgive you, I am forgiving myself for believing we are separate. We are not separate; we are all connected. When I look at you, I am looking at another aspect of myself.

As Cindy points out, all you have to do to make history is to become your authentic soul-self. By actualizing your soul-self, you send out ripples of energy into the world that elevate the level of vibration of our collective human consciousness. We are the problem. We are also the solution. You don't have to fix other people to make the world a better place; all you must do is fix yourself. That is the most important work given to each of us, because by changing ourselves, we change the world.

—Richard Barrett, Author of *Love, Fear, and the Destiny of Nations*

introduction

As a culture, and as individuals, we suffer from a case
of mistaken identity. This is not just one more problem
to add to our confusion—it is the central issue.

—PHILIP SHEPHERD, *NEW SELF, NEW WORLD*

As a global village, we have come a long way—from dwelling in caves to dwelling in condos, from horse-driven buggies to horse-powered cars, from the dark ages to an age where information travels at the speed of light. Despite humanity's great achievements and revolutionary breakthroughs, despite our millennia of progress and artistic heights, and despite century after century of luminous visionaries—men and women endowed with incredible insight into how this world works—the primary problem we face today as we emerge from the dawn of the third millennium is that we still have a very poor understanding of who we really are and what we are truly capable of. We have yet to recognize our collective genius and individual capacity for greatness.

As a species, we have been treading a rocky path, a circuitous pilgrimage toward authentic selfhood. We are just learning that the true wealth of a nation is not hidden in gold, diamond, or oil mines—but in its people. A *nation* is comprised of and defined by groups of people, not the geographical boundaries they live within. So while a country is bound by its topography, a nation rises or falls on the character of its people and the strength of its society.

In the early part of the 20th century, University of Kansas Chancellor E. H. Lindley stated, "We are in the midst of a revolution, and we are never going to be the same again. We have been riding in a vehicle of social thinking that is 100 years old, and we will have to change."[1] Those words still ring as true today. Nearly a hundred years ago, Lindley observed:

> The community and nation are new frontiers, where people
> are finding new ways to live together, for the good of all. Our
> children, we hope, as they face the future, will develop the
> spirit of the old pioneers, who were not afraid of new problems.[2]

I firmly believe that the younger generations of today are now those pioneers of new ways to live together. It was a decade or so after Lindley spoke those words that a young Napoleon Hill published his seminal, *Think and Grow Rich*, in the midst of the Great Depression. In this work, he writes:

> Never has there been a time more favorable to pioneers than
> the present. While most leaders manage the present, the real
> champions of our world are those who dare to craft a new and
> brighter future. True, there is no wild and wooly west to be
> conquered, as in the days of the Covered Wagon; but there is
> a vast business, financial, and industrial world to be remolded
> and redirected along new and better lines.[3]

Does this not ring true now more than ever? We are living in the aftermath of one of our country's worst economic disasters since the stock market crash of 1929. The same mechanism that brought the country to its knees then is what we saw repeated in the first decade of the 21st century: we were self-deceived. We did not face the truth about an economy built on falsehood—and that deception crippled our society for a decade. We must be willing to look as in a mirror at what we are seeing reflected in our institutions, political systems, and social structures. We must turn what we see reflected in the news and media back toward ourselves. The problem is not somewhere "out there" with some vague and ever-changing "them" (or Adam Smith's "invisible hand")—but perhaps this pervasive lack of integrity lies within ourselves. Could this "disintegration" we see in the world around us be a result of our own inner lives unraveling?

I believe the last and greatest frontier of exploration is not outer space, but inner space. Unchecked, unexplored, and undervalued, we will become the proverbial blind leading the blind—not because the truth is so difficult to know but because as a rule, we have an incredible tendency to get in our own and each other's way on the path to becoming who we should be: those who not only provoke history, but also shape it.

We live in a world tyrannized by partialities—by the drive to take the one part we know and make a whole out of it. Instead of living into the fullness of who we are becoming—pilgrims on a lifelong journey of learning and connecting—we instead settle down upon a singular point of enlightenment revealed along the way toward wholeness, spend the bulk of our time convincing others that it is the greatest of all discoveries, and build our castles and kingdoms there. We are then all too willing to live according to our imperfect understandings of even that one thing. You and I, as brilliant and gifted as we are, only know in part. Even the most educated among us possess a "degree" of information—be it a bachelor's, master's, or other tertiary degree. It is humbling to know that there is so much more to uncover, to discover, and to learn.

We are captives of our own constructs—prisoners of our own perspectives. In essence, the issues we face in the world are not a matter of defeating illness, redistributing wealth, or coming up with more efficient ways to disburse natural resources and information—or even devising the perfect political system so that freedom is available to all. The challenge is instead to truly understand who we are, what we were created for, and how best to participate in being members of a global community.

What the world needs is not a better way of *doing*, but a better way of *being*. We need a fuller, more complete, more truthful paradigm. While the world's youth and underrepresented voices take to the streets in historical disruptions—as happened during movements such as the Arab Spring, Occupy Wall Street, Black Lives Matter, and the Women's March on Washington (repercussions from all of which are still being felt today)—we continue to miss the point: *we will never make the world a better place by merely transforming our institutions or political systems; we can do it only by transforming ourselves.*

At the same time, we must acknowledge that we are each a work in process. I don't have all the answers. What I know, I know in part—but I am on a journey to keep learning and engaging in open dialogue until the full picture is revealed. Each day I strive for a fuller understanding of how I might make a greater impact toward positive change upon the earth. I know what it is to live in poverty and obscurity in a small nation, and I know what it is to prosper and succeed in the most prosperous country on earth. In either instance, it is only by understanding who I am—my unique heritage as well as my defining hopes—that I am able to walk in the power of the divine agency that God has granted to every human being.

WE THE PEOPLE ARE PERSONS

"We the people," a phrase used by the Founding Fathers of the United States of America, was inspired by a quest to guard and defend the inalienable, God-given rights of a newly liberated people moved by incredible wisdom and foresight to inscribe a vision of freedom and prosperity into its very DNA. When I imagine a nation or a region or a world where communities and cities are thriving, I think of *individuals* who are thriving. Humanity isn't an anonymous mass but individual human beings beloved of God and endowed with His creative genius. Where every person is empowered to maximize their potential to fulfill their purpose, communities will thrive and nations will prosper. This vision must continue to be strengthened and perpetuated not just for America, but also for the entire world. Let this caveat empower each of us—that we who belong to this human family are led, governed, thrive, progress, and prosper only as we are able to make our voices heard. And when government fails us, we have the power to change how and by whom we are governed. This is the recipe for true national and global success.

When I think about what it means to succeed as a people, I believe the first success we must pursue is to become the person each of us was meant to be—problem solvers, visionaries, agents of change, innovators, and leaders. We should find no contentment in merely achieving and acquiring, but we must keep growing in our ability to serve. It's not just about my success or your success as individuals but about all of us succeeding together—moving beyond individual wealth to commonwealth and a more just society.

Interestingly, when Jesus came to the earth, His main goal was not only to heal society, but also to heal bodies, hearts, and minds. When hearts and minds are made healed and whole, societies are automatically healed and able to function as an integrated whole. When Jesus spoke of the Kingdom of Heaven, He was not trying to establish a new political movement—something He could have done had that been His goal. Instead, He wanted to deliver people from self-centered thinking and self-imposed limitations into a new paradigm of self-discovery—a new way of understanding the universe and each of our places within it.

Constantly, He was making statements such as, "You have heard it said this way, but I want you to know it is really like this," or "If you will live into what I am teaching you, you will know what is true and perfect, and that truth will set you free," or "I give you a new commandment; living in this world is not about rigid legalism and lording yourself over others, it is about love. Do you want to be great? Then you must be the servant of all."[4] In essence, He was saying, "A new paradigm I give to you, a new way of being. Walk in this, and all you ever need to know will be provided—all your needs will be met, and you will live a life beyond your greatest dreams."

I also find it interesting that if you look in the Book of Acts, you'll see that it was a considerable amount of time before the followers of Jesus were referred to as "Christians." Initially, the disciples called following Jesus "The Way," a term oddly reminiscent of the Eastern concept of Taoism—not living rigidly according to a system of laws, but seeking to be in harmony with a flow, such as the rhythm of nature or the *"unforced rhythms of grace"* of which Jesus spoke.[5] This flow comes from the soul and is a celebration and appreciation of being in tune with one's innermost self.[6]

The early disciples had no initial desire to separate following Jesus from their understanding of Judaism or to turn it into an anti-Roman revolution; they wanted to teach people how to, as Paul put it, "walk in step with the Spirit of God."[7] It was not a religion with set practices and rituals that would become hollow and meaningless over time, but a way of living in syncopated rhythm—seeking to be in the flow of the Spirit of God, hearing from Him at all times, and continually being able to draw from the unlimited resources of Heaven for the transformation of life on earth.

To live in this way—the way we were created to live—is to walk in the paradigm of Heaven, not the limitations of the earth. It means understanding who we truly are, learning to be whole and healthy people delivered from the corruption that comes through imperfect and partial understandings of reality, and then tapping into the creative, transformational power of God to unleash that same quest in the lives of others.

But it also means meeting people where they are and being open to learning from their understandings as much as being willing to teach them from our own. For the truth is—despite what we see as differences—we are more a part of one another than anyone in a prior era has ever realized. We will never be all that we can be without a deep and wholehearted connection to others—and there are others out there who can never be all they were intended without a deep and wholehearted connection to us. Our strength is found in our diversity, and our destiny is determined by our harmony.

IN SEARCH OF WHOLENESS

In the following pages, I have attempted to compile much of what I have learned on my own personal journey in the hope of enabling you to more fully embrace yours and wholly express God's divine purpose for your life. You must realize that there are riches from God locked up within you—riches meant for you, but even more for the world around you. Understanding and releasing these things is a journey through the Bible, religion, philosophy, science, and metaphysics. While none of these present a complete understanding of reality in and of themselves—or our individual role within it—I believe each offers keys to the doors we must open on the way to becoming our most authentic and powerful selves.

This is a journey that starts with the "self," for it is from this reference point that our perception of the world and our significance in it begins. It is a journey that first wanders inward to heal and free so that what emerges out of us into the wider world can do the same. We cannot simply plaster acts of kindness over corrupt souls and believe it will do the world any good. Motives matter as much as ends. What Jesus came to teach was that world transformation begins with personal transformation. It is the path into a life of the limitlessness of Heaven—for the Heaven that we pray will envelop the earth is found within each of us.[8]

Of course, manifesting that Kingdom within our souls is no easy task, or more of us would be living in that beautiful reality every day of our lives. But what the message of the Kingdom does offer is a hope we can grasp hold of in any given moment. That hope is what anchors our souls and what compels us to break down the barriers to wholeness within our lives as well as within our communities.[9] Hope emboldens us and stirs our faith—a faith that is made effective only by love.[10]

It is Christ's love for us and working in and through us that compels us to action.[11] It is what calls us to a higher hope not only for ourselves, but also for those less fortunate—the vulnerable, displaced, and poor among us, whether across the world or across the street. And this call to action—the sum of "numberless diverse acts of courage and belief"— is what shapes history.[12]

The faith and courage required to shape history is grounded in hope, fueled by hope, and sustained by hope. Hebrews tells us, *"Faith is the substance of things hoped for"*—or *"shows the reality of what we hope for"*—so before such a reality appears, we must first hope.[13]

Now more than ever, it seems, the world is in need of hope and the wholeness it promises. *Wholeness*—or *whole*—is defined as "containing all components; complete. Not divided or disjoined. Not wounded, injured, or impaired: sound or unhurt. Having been restored; healed."[14]

As a nation and as a global community, we are more divided than at any other time in history. That divisiveness has not only caused a pervasive political paralysis, but it also threatens the very fabric of our society—and not just in the United States, but in every nation of the world. Our fractured governments and social structures, however, are only a symptom of a deeper splintering—a deeper woundedness, incompleteness, or "impairment," as the definition describes above.

If we are to restore and heal the nations of the world, we must first restore and heal the people within those nations. *The Merriam-Webster Dictionary* defines *wholeness* as not only "the condition of being sound in body," but also "the quality or state of being without restriction, exception, or qualification."[15] In other words, living without being excluded, constrained, or limited by any means such as background, culture, education, economics, beliefs, or fears—being free to realize our fullest potential as influencers, change catalysts, and creative forces for good.

This is hope in action; it is the fruit of a restored and healed soul. When we are enabled to heal our souls, we are empowered to heal the world. We move out from under social, cultural, or psychological constraints to help others do the same, who then in turn help others:

Each time a man stands up for an ideal, or acts
to improve the lot of others, or strikes out against injustice,
he sends forth a tiny ripple of hope.

—ROBERT F. KENNEDY

SAVED BY HOPE

Bobby Kennedy understood the power of hope. Like a spark that catches fire, he believed that as long as hope flickered, there would be light—and that even a little bit of light could dispel the darkness. He referred to those flickers of light as "centers of energy" that when crossed from a million directions with one another, create an unstoppable force: "Those ripples build a current, which can sweep down the mightiest walls of oppression and resistance," wrote Kennedy.[16]

In his short life, Kennedy shaped history. His hope and character continue to speak into the lives of today's activists and inform our nation's greatest leaders. Ronald Reagan said of him, "He aroused the comfortable. He exposed the corrupt, remembered the forgotten, inspired his countrymen, and renewed and enriched the American conscience."[17]

Today, we need voices of hope to inspire, renew, and enrich the American conscience—as well as that of other nations. We need individuals who will carry that hope to those who have lost hope. We need to be willing to do the work within ourselves that will enable us to dream bigger, think more expansively, and conceive of new possibilities—to imagine what has not yet been but *could be*, and then doggedly believe that it *can be*.

It is time to start learning what we are truly capable of—who we were created and put into the universe to be at this time in history. Could you be the answer someone is looking for? Are you in possession of a missing piece to a puzzling situation or problem? Could it be found hidden within your soul—that nugget of insight or wisdom or revelation the world so desperately needs? Could it be the Christ in you, a hurting world's hope of experiencing God's beauty and goodness—His majesty and glory?[18]

His name will be the hope of all the world.[19]

We are the carriers of the peace the world seeks, but how can we as the Body of Christ, or as its individual members, impart that peace if it continues to personally elude *us*?[20] We must establish the Kingdom we wish to see spread across the globe within *our own* hearts first of all—in all righteousness, peace, and joy—with all faith, hope, and love—our hearts established in peace, complete, and lacking nothing.[21] Only when we are able to live and lead from this place of wholeness will we be poised to mend our fragmented world.

For this reason, we will begin this journey by dealing with the realm of your soul from where hope emanates. If we are to shape history, or even our own lives, we must first give hope a place to ripple from.

It is my prayer that as you read this book, you will stir the waters of your hidden potential until you are able to make those ripples become waves. I pray you will take major strides down the path toward wholeness and begin living fully into the promise of your destiny—and that when you begin to walk in the fullness of that life day by day, the world will be transformed by your transformation and the dreams you are now able to dream. It is a journey of the soul; it is a journey of discovery—and it is the only journey that really matters.

There are those who look at things the way they are and ask, "Why?"...I dream of things that never were and ask, "Why not?"

—ROBERT F. KENNEDY

Every great movement for social change has been animated by people who did serious inner work to constellate, consolidate, and give trajectory to the powers of the human heart.

Only by taking the inner life seriously and learning how to access and aim that power that is in us—not only individually but collectively—could any of these great movements for change have happened.

The capacity to take the inner life seriously and to tap the sources of power that lie within us...are as important in the transformation of institutions and societies as any of the external powers that we give so much credit to.

Our theory of change begins with that work of individual transformation.

—PARKER PALMER, *HEALING THE HEART OF DEMOCRACY*

PART ONE

CREATING RIPPLES OF HOPE

I am only one,
But still I am one.
I cannot do everything,
But still I can do something;
And because I cannot do everything,
I will not refuse to do the something that I can do.

—EDWARD EVERETT HALE, "I AM ONLY ONE"

CHAPTER ONE

the heart of the problem

Here, longing for the refuge of his mother's arms, stands a hungry two-year-old—not a number to be "processed." Who is going to care for him? No. That is the wrong question. Am I going to care for him? Will I pick him up, wrap my blanket around him, be his advocate with the Rwandan military, and find him food, water, and shelter?

—DARROW L. MILLER, *DISCIPLING NATIONS*

As long as one child is hungry, our lives will be filled with anguish and shame. What all these victims need above all is to know that they are not alone; that we are not forgetting them, that when their voices are stifled we shall lend them ours, that while their freedom depends on ours; the quality of our freedom depends on theirs.

—ELIE WIESEL, NOBEL PEACE PRIZE
ACCEPTANCE SPEECH

The degree to which one is sensitive to other people's
suffering, to other people's humanity, is the
index of one's own humanity.

—ABRAHAM JOSHUA HESCHEL, *WHO IS MAN?*

In his documentary *I Am*, filmmaker Tom Shadyac poses two questions to authors and thinkers the world over: 1) "What's wrong with the world?" and 2) "What can we do about it?"[1] After taking his audiences on a journey that spans science, religion, and philosophy, he quotes what author G. K. Chesterton wrote in an essay when asked by London's *The Times* newspaper "What's wrong with the world?" Chesterton's response came in the form of a letter consisting of one line: "Dear Sir, I am. Yours, G.K. Chesterton."

As we look at the world in the early hours of the third millennium AD—one more rife with technology and innovation than any other in the history of humanity—we realize that, despite what we have accomplished, we are no wiser, contemporarily speaking, than people were before the dawn of the industrial age. For all our progress, we have made but small strides in ending hatred, the dominance of fear in our lives, war, and exploitation. Slavery and human bondage are at an all-time high and are surprisingly prevalent even in the most advanced regions of the Western world. Many believe we are no better off as human beings for our industrial and information technology than we were centuries ago. While we gain dominion over the natural world, we are little by little losing connection with our own souls. I believe we have misdiagnosed the pain we are feeling as the problem. The pain is only an indication of a much deeper soul issue—humanity's search for meaning and purpose.

The human innovative intellect has never been greater since the time Thomas Edison invented the light bulb and the phonograph (I wonder what Edison would think of an iPhone?), but the health of our souls has never been in more peril. The divide between rich and poor grows deeper by the day, while the small percentage of the world's wealthy consumes a grossly disproportional amount of the world's natural resources. Because of the demand for consumer goods, there are more slaves today than were ever taken out of Africa and other parts of the world in the history of slavery—an estimated 27 million people—and 40 to 50 percent of these are children.

Human trafficking is now rivaling drug and weapons sales as the most profitable form of syndicated crime. Many within these numbers are women and children who are raped repeatedly day after day in the growing sex trade. Other children are taken from their families and conscripted into wars they are too young to understand. Despite advances in agriculture and food production, famines still devastate vast regions of the world. Poverty is growing—and those affected by diseases such as AIDS find little reprieve from revolutionary new treatments they can't afford. In other areas of the world, admitting you are of one religion or another can get you killed, imprisoned, or tortured.

Hatred between ethnic groups has existed for centuries, yet despite our greater understanding of human psychology and appreciation of cultural diversity, we are no closer to resolving conflicts and achieving peace in our schools, neighborhoods, cities, or nations than we were decades ago. If anything, things have gotten worse rather than better. And as the various factions of those conflicts arm themselves with weapons—even weapons of mass destruction—the future seems precarious. As Albert Einstein once said, "I know not with what weapons World War III will be fought, but World War IV will be fought with sticks and stones."

Add to this the growing malaise gripping the nations of the world as economic and political environments become more volatile. In December 2010, an unemployed college graduate was arrested for trying to sell fruit on a street corner in Tunisia in order to make a little money. The reason? He didn't have a permit as a street vendor. Driven to desperation because he could find neither a job nor a way to provide for himself, the young man lit himself on fire as a protest against the oppressive policies of President Zine al-Abidine Ben Ali and his government.[2] According to a CNN report, the fatal protest unleashed a wave of regional dissent against oppression, government corruption, and stifled freedoms.[3] While regime officials lived lavishly, the unemployment rate was at an unprecedented high, and far too many struggled to put food on the table for their families and themselves.

Within hours of this young man's suicide, Tunisia was turned upside down by rioting that eventually forced Ben Ali to step down and flee the country. This spark ignited a wildfire that spread across northern Africa and into the Middle East as discontented citizens rose up against the corruption and excesses of their governments. Within weeks, Hosni Mubarak also stepped down from power in Egypt. Protests broke out among the people of Jordan, Yemen, Bahrain, Algeria, Libya, Iran, and Syria, many of whom were violently suppressed. Muammar Gaddafi was forced from power by a bloody civil war and finally killed after more than 2,000 were slaughtered by his government forces. While many heralded these events as battles for freedom and democracy, the aftermath is not looking so bright. Nor was the unrest confined to simply one region or the nations of one certain political philosophy. Riots also broke out in the birthplace of democracy, Greece, in response to austerity measures adopted to deal with that nation's crippling debt—and then in England, as racial and socio-economic differences led to protests and looting. Now Brexit threatens to isolate Britain from the rest of Europe.

Perhaps you, as I do, shake your head at such things and wonder what can be done. While we have a greater means of helping one another than we've ever had before, why do things continue to get worse for so many? Why the quick tendency to violence and the gross neglect of the developing world? How can we feature ten-million-dollar weddings on magazine covers and new multi-billion-dollar megaplexes in our nightly news, yet give so little attention to the billions who don't have access to clean water? How is it that so many still grow up abused and neglected and needy in a world that has such abundance?

It's easy to point fingers at governments, societies, and the rich as the causers of all the ills of the world, and it is likely there are probably those who deserve a good portion of the blame, but we can't miss the wisdom of what Mr. Chesterton shared in his two-word answer. What's wrong with the world? *I am*. I will make little difference in the world if I only blame others for what is happening. I can throw myself at the problems of the world and spend a lifetime trying to solve them, but if in the end *I am* no more intellectually and emotionally healthy than anyone else, all I do is replace the corruption of others with my own. As Mahatma Gandhi is popularly credited as stating, you and I must "be the change" we desire to see manifested in the world.

Though I myself still have a lot of room for growth in many areas, my life has been one of trying to live to be the change I wish to see in the world from the inside of my soul outward to everyone I can reach around me. Despite being raised in poverty by a single mother in Bermuda, I refused to be a statistic. I was the sixth child of seven, and there were days we ran out of everything, including water. Though we were poor, my mother didn't let poverty define how we lived. She worked hard to keep us all in clothes, fed, and furnished with school supplies, but it was tough for one person to keep up with the needs of eight. Rather than wallow in depression about what we didn't have, she inspired me to think like an entrepreneur to provide the "extras" I longed for, whether that meant new shoes or ballet lessons. I developed self-discipline and prized the rewards of hard work even from a very young age. Despite having everything against us, I found a way to get the education I needed to take me from the dispirited realm of poverty to the halls of parliamentary leadership.

Fresh out of college, I landed a job in the Department of Education. Seeing the need, I helped initiate a program to address drug and alcohol abuse, sat on a government-appointed Women's Advisory Committee, and was part of a multi-disciplinary team of consultants and advisors formed for the purpose of addressing educational challenges that laid the foundation for national reforms. Subsequently, gaining the attention of the premier of Bermuda, I became a senator. I served in that capacity for a time, but at the end of my term I realized people needed more than programs or policies if real change was to be made.

Driven by the conviction that people need to be transformed from the inside out and that they need, more than anything else, the revolutionary spiritual awakening that only a relationship with the living God provides, I decided to lay aside working through the external constructs of corporations and governments to work instead to change the internal constructs of hearts and minds. I wanted to be part of changing nations and generations so that, just as I had experienced in my own life, people around the world could experience authentic empowerment that would help take them from socio-economic poverty and poverty of the soul to positions of influence, spreading positive change wherever they went.

In many ways, this book is a culmination of what I have learned along the way, what I am working on now, where I hope to be, and what I hope to do in the years to come—life lessons inherently yet precariously dangling like keys divinely designed to unlock inner healing and also empower you to be the change you desire to see in your world.

Let me start by explaining where I come from personally. Hopefully, you can take what I am saying and translate it into something meaningful for you, rather than reject it because you feel it is skewed or opinionated. I admit up front that I don't know everything, and despite my best efforts, a great deal of me is still a product of my beliefs and background—but I also know that just because your beliefs and background are different, that doesn't mean we can't learn from each other. Beliefs can divide, but values will unite, and when we value the same things, we can learn from one another, even about our own faiths. How do I know? I know because I have learned incredible things from those outside my own heritage and faith traditions. If you are open, I believe you can learn a great deal from mine as well.

First of all, I think you should know that I am a Christian, a follower of the teachings and life of Jesus of Nazareth. When I was a young woman, I made a very conscious decision to become a Christian. I believe God provides incredible insights into understanding life, the universe, and everything it contains—and that God does exist and showed His great love for humanity just as the famous verse says:

For God so loved the world, that He gave His only Son [Jesus], that whoever believes in Him should not perish but have eternal life. For God did not send His Son into the world to condemn the world, but in order that the world might be saved through Him.[4]

This is the God who influenced three of my heroes—Mohandas Gandhi, Martin Luther King Jr., and Mother Teresa. This is the God who has influenced and empowered me. I want to be open about this because I want you to understand that the paradigm taught by Christ is what shapes and liberates my world. It is this framework that I will be using in this book to describe what I believe reveals who we are, why we are here, and what it all means. To me, the teachings of Jesus Christ epitomize key principles for life and living.

These principles are summarized in the words of civil rights activist Vincent Harding:

> Once we see the fact that we are members of a human community, once we use the idea of community as that which joins us together, then there is no mystery about the fact that our best development as individuals is tied intrinsically to the best development of the community at large, and that the community has as its major responsibility the development of the best possibilities of its members. And its members have as their great responsibility the best development of the community.[5]

Dr. Harding goes on to show how this same principle is the foundation upon which the *United* States of America was built:

> That is what is in the Preamble to our Constitution. Remember, it says, "We the people of the United States, in order to form a more perfect union…" That is our job as the people of the United States—not to create the best technology in the world, not to create more bombs than anybody else or more drones, but our job is to create a more perfect

community, a more perfect union: what King used to call the beloved community. If we can understand that that is deeply embedded in our very reason for being, then there is no contradiction between the development of the person and the development of the community.[6]

This was the primary principle upon which America was founded over 200 years ago and allowed Christianity to flourish for over 2,000 years—yet in spite of having built a nation and Church upon this premise of "a more perfect union," it remains a concept that largely eludes us today. What are we, as a people of *"like precious faith,"* who are called above all else to be of one heart and mind, doing within our spheres of influence to promote a more perfect community among the wider human family?[7]

Many would look at the history of Christianity and ascribe most of the ills we see in the world to its influence. However, you don't have to look too far to find that there are more orphanages and hospitals started by men and women who chased after God than great politicians or military conquerors. I deeply believe that it is our spiritual attributes that inspire us to be and to do good. I am also firmly convinced that until we can face and disarm—on a daily basis—the selfishness and corruption of our own souls, we will never be able to do the same in the world around us. In essence, however you want to frame it, the battle for the earth is first a spiritual one. Good deeds can only be done out of good hearts; otherwise, they end up empty and eventually twisted to the wrong purposes.

Although my thinking is informed by the faith tradition that I understand and embrace, I trust that you will benefit from the conversation I'm inviting you into here—even if your faith background is different from mine. I believe that if you will keep an open mind and allow what I share here to speak to your heart, it will add to your understanding of who God is and how He designed us to live as a community in peace and harmony rather than strife and discord.

The world into which we were born no longer exists. The world in which we live is a place characterized by economic uncertainties, geo-political volatilities, and leadership gaps—a world filled with more questions and conundrums than answers. Yet it is precisely because of these very things that we find ourselves in a world offering more opportunity than ever before. While it is a place of increasing crime, poverty, substance abuse, corruption, exploitation, and a host of other ills, it is also a time of unprecedented advancement for goodwill, beauty, discovery, innovation, prosperity, connectivity, fulfillment, and joy.

In the last handful of centuries, humanity has used science and reason, innovation and technology, to transform our planet into the stuff that was science fiction only decades ago, but such progress has come with its costs as well. Though science and industry have been powerful tools in the hands of brilliant men and women, they are reaching their limits. We can no longer afford to produce and consume our world's natural resources and toss out toxic pollutants as we did throughout the 20th century without threatening the very survival of life on earth. We can no longer sustain boom and bust capitalist consumerism as the answer to every problem without facing another Great Depression that will circle the world in mere hours—and within days put millions out of work, laying the foundation for greater unrest and violence. We can't continue to believe everything will be alright if we keep doing the same things we have done in the past. We are not going to get different results from making the same mistakes.

We need new answers for a new age. We need a new paradigm for being caretakers of our planet, each other, and ourselves. We need to find a way to heal our individual souls so that we can each be transformed from the inside out. We need a fresh spiritual awakening. While science can give us new methods and breakthroughs in its practice, true creativity and innovation comes from the spiritual realm. While the natural realm is a place of limitations, the spiritual realm is a place of unlimited possibilities—where what was once thought impossible will discover its realization and be birthed in the natural world as a life-giving force. We can no longer just be masters of the physical world; we must also understand who we are as spiritual beings and how to access the answers that only God can give us. But how do we get the answers we need from the spiritual, creative realm for the problems our world faces in the physical, natural realm?

All true innovators—scientific, political, social, and otherwise—have always been men and women who knew how to reach inside for answers, even if they didn't exactly know how they were doing it. Sir Isaac Newton's greatest work was not defining the law of gravity, but a commentary on the Bible. The deeper Einstein dug into physics, the more he realized there had to be a God. Some of his most profound statements are not mathematical, but spiritual and moral. Gandhi spent more time in prayer than making speeches. Johannes Gutenberg's motivation for inventing the printing press was that all might have access to what he believed was the Word of God. Science and industry bring wonderful, powerful change, but it is from the spirit that we create and find answers that have no negative side effects. It's not just about making advancements; it is also about living in a way that benefits all. As the 1995 winner of the Templeton Prize—an award that "honors a living person who has made an exceptional contribution to affirming life's spiritual dimension, whether through insight, discovery, or practical works"—Arizona State University professor and researcher Paul Davies put it:

> All the early scientists such as Newton were religious in one way or another. They saw their science as a means of uncovering traces of God's handiwork in the universe. What we now call the laws of physics they regarded as God's abstract creation: thoughts, so to speak, in the mind of God. So in doing science, they supposed, one might be able to glimpse the mind of God.[8]

This book is not about religion; it is about knowing God intimately enough to communicate with Him and discern the solutions He wants to give us. Religions are really about practices and rituals—habits and methods, if you will—that help us open ourselves up to more fully knowing and hearing from God. The problem is, at the same time, their practice alone can be mistaken as knowing God and what is right. As the famous atheist Richard Dawkins said in an interview with *The New York Times*, "Religion teaches you to be satisfied with nonanswers. It's sort of a crime against childhood."[9] I believe that is an astonishingly valid observation, because when I got rid of religion and placed more emphasis on a relationship with God, it was only then that I found God. It is often too easy to substitute—or mistake—external practice for internal connection to the expanse of the spiritual—to the true nature of reality. I have no interest in teaching religion here; what I want to do is explore what is spiritual and see how we can learn together from that investigation. There are things we have to learn from one another, and I believe the only way we will be able to discover them is by sharing our ideas.

So, whatever your background, I believe that there are things you can learn here that will help you better understand how to have a relationship with the infinite God—a relationship that is more about communicating with Him than trying to please Him in the hopes He will bless your life and your work and one day reward you with a wonderful afterlife. God has better plans for you than you do for yourself, but they won't come without your participation. The choices we make—consciously or unconsciously—from what we know and believe direct our lives, whether we like it or not.

Our first step is to explore the power of what we believe at its most basic roots. The fundamental question that rings in my heart is, "Is what we believe helping us or hindering us?" The first step toward being what we were created to be is very often, literally, changing our minds.

We must do everything we can to encourage imagination…
to dream impossible dreams and to know that [we] have the
capacity within [ourselves] to create something better.

—Vincent Harding

Once again we are invited to remember that our inner
and outer worlds are mirrors of each other. It is the
simplicity of this single memory that allows miracles...
to be expected rather than hoped for.

—GREGG BRADEN, *THE ISAIAH EFFECT*

History maker arise...and reflect on how you are the solution!

Reflect on the question that was presented to G. K. Chesterton: *What's wrong with the world?* Then, craft a response based on *your* gifts, talents, and passions. Don't rush through the process too quickly. Think about it carefully. Everything God has entrusted you with is meant to be stewarded—*and then released!*

When Chesterton claimed personal responsibility for what was wrong with the world, he was not making a statement of defeat; he was taking ownership of the possibility that *he* could likewise carry and release solutions to the chaos around him.

We have received the assignment of dominion; this Genesis mandate was never revoked or reversed. If anything, it was *reinforced* because Jesus reclaimed this authority from the powers of darkness at His resurrection and now gives "whosoever will" the opportunity to arise and design the world that they want to see.

History maker arise...and pray for Heaven's solutions to be entrusted to you.

At the end of each chapter, there is a simple prayer directive that will help you discuss these critical points with God. Remember, prayer is not a monologue; it's a dialogue. It's an exchange between Heaven and earth.

Perhaps the most famous prayer of all is, *"Your Kingdom come, Your will be done, on earth as it is in Heaven."*[10] Consider how you might bring certain aspects of Heaven to earth based on your unique proclivities. What needs are you especially passionate about? What causes move you to action?

Ask God, your Creator, to open your eyes to the solutions you alone carry to the injustices He shows you.

CHAPTER TWO

ideas have consequences

You will know the truth, and the truth will set you free.

—JOHN 8:32

*Whether you think you can, or you think
you can't—you're right.*

—HENRY FORD

It is fundamental to human nature that truth matters, even if we have little idea of what it really is. People who are atheists can be radical evangelists of their "non-belief"—adamant to convince others of their "truth," which they feel is important for everyone to accept, even if, in the end, they believe that life is ultimately meaningless. To them, their truth that God doesn't exist is more important than people finding fulfillment in false beliefs.

No matter what we believe, in the end, we are all wired to be governed by our belief system—and are convinced that holding to those beliefs is what truly matters. When we find our place of truth, we find our place of freedom. After all, we must have a context for understanding the universe and a paradigm through which we filter the mass of information that bombards our minds on a daily basis, lest we find ourselves awash in a turbulent sea of stimuli without an anchor as prisoners of ignorance and intolerance. If there really were no God, then what would it matter if someone believed in one? Why not leave them to their so-called "delusion"?

The reason is basic—at our core, we hold truth to be of primal importance, even if the truth we hold is that "truth" doesn't exist.

Though it is somewhat based in the egotistical need to be right, it is more than that. We cannot really understand anything in our world without an overarching construct within which to place it. How we see reality affects how we behave on every level, and it determines both a society's and an individual's level of prosperity and self-empowerment or poverty and complacent acceptance of the status quo.

Scholars call this a *worldview* or a *mental model*. Social scientists call it a *paradigm*. As Darrow Miller defines it in his book on the subject:

> A worldview is a set of assumptions held consciously or unconsciously in faith about the basic makeup of the world and how it works.[1]

Whether we realize it or not, we each have a worldview we have developed from childhood that either hinders us or helps us. We garnered it from socialization, culturalization, education, and our relational constellation. Your worldview determines the constructs of your reality—your perception of belonging, whether what you do or don't do really matters, what in life is worth working for, why you are here, who you are, how you treat others, how you allow others to treat you, and what is or isn't acceptable in terms of health, living conditions, happiness, and a myriad of other standards. How you perceive reality affects every aspect of your life. What you believe not only aligns you with the true nature of existence, but it also aligns the true nature of existence with you—what you believe actually affects reality. Belief systems define the cultures of the earth and the economic and physical well-being of every society. As Miller puts it, "Ideas have consequences."[2]

When Jesus came to earth preaching about the coming of a new kingdom—the Kingdom of God or the Kingdom of Heaven—He was, in fact, trying to spread a new worldview. He was trying to shift people's paradigms. The reality they knew was based on dog-eat-dog conquest and exploitation, but He wanted to teach them a reality based on selfless love and personal empowerment. These are principles that have been at war with one another as long as human beings have been on the earth: Do we take, or do we share? Do we fight, or do we tolerate? Do we dominate, or do we cooperate? Do we exploit, or do we empower?

Why does this matter? Because whatever is keeping you from your dreams is something you don't yet know, something you haven't yet done, or a discipline you haven't yet built into your life. And what is keeping you from making this breakthrough? Too often it is your personal worldview. You are missing that key bit of wisdom because your worldview isn't open to finding or accepting what that might be. Your answer could bite you on your nose, but if your worldview is wrong, you won't recognize it for what it is—you won't be open to accepting it.

Thus the question is not "What is the one thing I need to know or receive?" but "Am I open to learning, and am I on the right path to discovery and discipline?" If you are, then what you need will come to you, and the change could transform you from an employee to an employer, from someone on welfare to the founder of a fund that sends others to college and supports nonprofits working to end poverty. The change can be so dramatic that the rest of the world will see you as an overnight success, even though you have spent years in focused pursuit.

Overarching worldviews tend first to be based in the nature of the universe as we know it. Is all that is real only what we experience with our five physical senses, or is there something beyond that? Did all that now exists come from a tiny atom, or is there another realm out of which everything materialized? Which is the true realm?

Most worldviews are based in a dualistic relationship between two realms: 1) the physical or natural and 2) the spiritual or supernatural. This allows for four different perspectives:

1. All that we sense with our five senses is all that exists (the secular and scientific view).

2. All that is in the physical world is illusion (animist and Eastern philosophy).

3. There is a spiritual and a physical realm, but they have little interaction with one another (gnostic or legalistic).

4. Both realms exist and have continual interaction with one another, even though one was created by the other (theistic).

While there are varying degrees of worldviews that would fit between these broad definitions, these are the four poles that ultimately define all religions, philosophies, and systematic explanations of the nature of reality. To one extent or another, they also define how cultures prosper and innovate.

If, for example, you believe that this natural world is really just temporary and substantially an illusion, why would you work to build anything in it? If it were all about enduring this life as best you can so that you can be born into a higher level in the next, why would you fight the status quo? Such a struggle would ultimately be counterproductive and would actually inhibit your eventual fulfillment rather than help it. The individual only really matters in relationship to the whole as a cog working to maintain things as they are. Cultures that embrace this as their basic worldview are some of the poorest and most populous in the world.

On the other hand, if you believe solely in a secular, material-only world, then humanity's answers can come only from human beings. Prayer, spiritual formation, and all religious pursuits are empty and meaningless. Solutions will come through political policies and ideologies, science, the justice system, the redistribution of resources, revolution/war, and/or diplomacy. We are on our own and responsible only to ourselves. Free from the ethical, creative reality of the spiritual world, however, these systems are only as good as the people in them, many of whom are corrupt and looking more to promote themselves and their livelihood than the causes they say they are endorsing. When push comes to shove, their own lives and well-being are all that matter.

Human beings are fickle and imperfect as it is, but left to ourselves without God, corruption can't help but seep into everything we do, and that corruption ultimately compromises our best intentions. Though we don't make a conscious decision to do wrong, it is unavoidable if we acknowledge no authority in our lives higher than our own self.

Truth be told, it is very unlikely that the worldview we hold is one that we have consciously chosen in the first place. Cultures are rich with paradigm-forming "subliminal messages" that are in what we read, listen to, and see. They seep into our minds without us realizing it from even the most reputable of sources, and without analysis or understanding we let them form the foundational principles of our worlds to the point that we disregard truths that contradict our mistaken worldviews, even when they hit us full in the face. We form mind-sets that are fixed in concrete, have certain expectations of the universe, and then our experiences follow that course. Our conclusions are rooted in our constructs.

Now, it's not an absolute cause and effect, as is sometimes suggested in the modern repackaging of old teachings, such as *The Secret* or *The Power of Positive Thinking*, but there is a connection too entangled to be denied. Having positive thoughts won't bring *only* positive things, but correcting our thinking is the place to start. It's not mystical hocus pocus, but it *is* spiritual (and also pragmatic). Conversely, people tend to throw the baby out with the bathwater, seeing excess in one area and assuming everything related to it is mistaken. They hear of a distortion about "positive thinking" or some such philosophy and assume it is all a ruse or a delusion. By doing this they miss out on the very change they need to make because it is not part of their faith system or scientific reasoning. They then bite the very hand with which God is trying to feed them.

This is why it is so important to examine what you believe and how it is helping or hampering your God-ordained destiny. The ideas we accept have ramifications, even though the effects may take years to realize. Our belief that our fate is sealed, that we are on our own, that whatever we try to do will never amount to anything—or any number of other defeatist attitudes that we acquiesce to without thinking too deeply—can easily block us from all we were intended to be. The problem is, if we truly recognized these mind-sets for what they are, we would reject them—but mind-sets are difficult to adjust precisely because they are difficult to recognize. They lay buried in our subconscious like the foundation under a house—I mean, we get all excited about the rooms and décor but don't realize that if the foundation is bad, the house is not worth living in. Not only that, but we accept these views without much thought or analysis, and thus, we live by them without much thought or analysis. We truly must dig in and think for a change. We must choose to think differently if we are to live differently—to give our thoughts some mindful consideration in order to be conscious of where they are taking us.

Finding your place of truth has the power not only to change you, but also to cause ordinary people facing extraordinary challenges to do extraordinary things.

Contracting AIDS through a blood transfusion, hemophiliac Ryan White, an Indiana teen who eventually passed away at the age of eighteen, became the new face of the deadly epidemic, debunking the atrocious notion that this disease was a curse placed upon drug users and those who were sexually promiscuous. His fight for fair treatment within the public school system had a universal ripple effect.

Nobel Peace Prize winner, environmentalist, and political activist Dr. Wangari Maathai, founder of the Green Belt Movement, discerned her truth in trees. "When we plant trees," she said, "we plant the seeds of peace and hope."[3] In an effort to empower rural women who reported their streams were drying up, their food supply was less secure, and that they had to walk further than ever before for firewood, this localized Kenyan movement caused a ripple effect that resulted in a worldwide movement on climate change in partnership with the United Nations Environment Program.

There are many amazing stories of ordinary people creating extraordinary change documented by the award-winning series *CNN Heroes*.[4] I was personally moved by the story of Jeison Aristizábal, the 2016 "Hero of the Year," who pioneered work helping people with disabilities in Colombia gain access to medical and educational resources. Jeison suffers from cerebral palsy but did not allow his own disability keep him from launching a foundation out of his parents' garage. After a decade and a half, his work has impacted the way his nation deals with disabilities, and he is now recognized internationally as a distinguished champion of change.

Recognizing a problem is the first step toward changing it. You see, while we must realize that there are issues of great concern in the world, it is even more important for us to recognize that there are answers as well. Those answers, however, will not come from sticking with "business as usual." We have to do things differently. Whether you supported him or not, when Barack Obama put "Change" and "Hope" on his campaign posters, he tapped into a national need that resonated with people enough that he rode that wave to the White House. While that change proved harder for him to deliver than anticipated, we would do well to follow his example of putting himself out there as an agent of change. However, there is no real hope if we do it in our own power; we must do it in the power of God. Neither is there hope if we try to do it when we are broken and incomplete ourselves. We have to heal ourselves so that we have the clout to heal our world.

Change doesn't come through programs or philosophies—it comes through people. Change is not just a process; it's a person who, in changing, becomes a catalyst of change. More specifically, it comes through people connecting with people, influencing and infecting one another with vision and inspiration and then moving forward together to infect others with that same remedy to hopelessness. The vision then grows as each individual adds her or his component to the whole. Without each piece, the picture would never be complete.

This kind of growth is dynamic and alive with possibility. It is powerful, but it is also fragile. Neglect and disconnection easily derail it. If it is groundbreaking, others will fight it, sometimes violently. Nor is it enough for a shared vision to just have a good start; it also needs a good ending, which will never happen unless it also has a good in-between. It takes foresight, courage, endurance, and creativity. It takes intelligence, knowledge, truth, and wisdom. It takes a village and more. And as much as it takes transformational leadership and transactional relationships, it also takes transformed paradigms—the "I" factor. It will take you and me having the courage to step forward from out of the shadows and bring to bear upon our challenges our piece of the puzzle. To do that, we must right our own ships, set our pioneering courses, and sail to where we are directed through the quiet tugs on our hearts by God—laden with the treasures to help others do the same.

We have to realize that we are living in a world full of possibilities. God created it to be that way, because from the start, He had great plans for us. Let's take a look at some of the things that God put into play from the very beginning. As we do, may they begin to form a new paradigm in you—one that will first heal your soul and then make you a healer of your world.

> *The world is certainly thought of as a place of spiritual trial,*
> *but it is also the confluence of soul and body, word and flesh,*
> *where thoughts must become deeds, where goodness must be*
> *enacted. This is the great meeting place, the narrow passage*
> *where spirit and flesh, word and world, pass into each other.*
>
> —WENDELL BERRY, *THE UNSETTLING OF AMERICA*

Hope is a choice in that we have this capacity to think about the future that's unique to human beings, and we build that capacity over time. It's a personal choice to either invest in thinking about the future and your expectations about what might happen or to let each day go by passively without really becoming an active agent in your own life.

—Dr. Shane Lopez

History maker arise...and find the power of your truth!

While living and breathing in this world, we are ever navigating the narrow straits of truth and error—which thoughts should become deeds and which should be forgotten. The world we live in isn't perfect, but it is the only meeting place we have—it is the space we inhabit between birth and death, the "narrow passage where spirit and flesh, word and world, pass into each other."

Reflect on the opportunities that have arisen in your life to widen the "narrow passage"—opportunities, for example, to reach people unaware of their own expansive potential. Where might God be positioning you to open hearts and minds to the "above-and-beyond-what-we-can-ask-or-imagine" power of Christ at work in them?

What do you believe to be true about what is possible for those around you? How can you live and breathe the power of this truth in your own life?

History maker arise...and pray for Heaven's truth to be revealed through you.

Because the world is the "confluence of soul and body, word and flesh, where thoughts must become deeds, where goodness must be enacted," you must believe that your actions matter. As James proclaimed centuries ago, *"Now someone may argue, 'Some people have faith; others have good deeds.' But I say, 'How can you show me your faith if you don't have good deeds? I will show you my faith by my good deeds.'"*[5]

Prayerfully consider how you might show *"yourself to be a pattern of good works"* as Paul instructed Titus.[6] Press into the Spirit of God as you seek to grow in grace and knowledge so you would neither stumble nor be unfruitful but would *"prove what is that good and acceptable and perfect will of God."*[7]

what frames your world?

The Lord by wisdom founded the earth;
By understanding He established the heavens;
By His knowledge the depths were broken up,
And clouds drop down the dew.

—PROVERBS 3:19–20 NKJV

The worlds were framed by the word of God, so that things
which are seen were not made of things which are visible.

—HEBREWS 11:3 NKJV

The first chapters of the Book of Genesis tell the Hebrew and Christian creation story. Whether you take this story literally or figuratively—whether you believe it describes the six 24-hour periods in which the universe was created, six huge epochs of time in which the earth was formed and came to be as it is today, or some other derivative of these two interpretations—this is much more than a parable of beginnings. As the very first words recorded by God to humanity, it is not just the outline of how God created the world we live in, but it also sets forth a framework for understanding and relating to a universe that is both substantive and celestial. It is a reality in which words contain enormous creative power and knowledge has a way of framing our understanding so that we can unlock the enormous potential of even the simplest of created things.

Take, for example, the life and work of a man like George Washington Carver. Born during the final years of the Civil War, young George never knew his father and was soon separated from his mother when a raiding party kidnapped them to keep them from being set free. George had had ten sisters and a brother who all died in childhood. Eventually George was saved when his former master, Moses Carver, arranged for him to be traded for a racehorse. Despite being saved from his kidnappers, he would never see his mother again. Moses and his wife raised George as their own son, but at age 13 he had to leave town if he wanted to attend school, as the local school did not allow African-American children to attend.

On his own in a land that was far from friendly to a clever young African American, George set out to make his mark on the world, knowing only two things: 1) that Jesus loved him enough to give His life for him, and 2) that he needed an education. Most who looked at that young boy must have said he didn't have a prayer, but as things turned out, that was all he really needed.

George put himself through school by his wits and work ethic. He never went anywhere without a book to read whenever he had a spare minute. From the time he was 12 until he graduated from college, he put in as many hours working each week as he did going to classes. At recess, instead of playing he would run to his job, work for a short time, and then make it back just as the bell rang. Every minute beyond being in class, working, and sleeping, he spent with his nose in a book.

By the time he graduated with a master's degree, he was one of the most coveted teachers and researchers in the United States. He could have accepted any number of posts that would have provided him with a comfortable life, but George wanted more. He looked at the state of African Americans in the South—most of them were sharecroppers barely eking out an existence—so rather than joining a prestigious faculty, George became one of the founding professors at Booker T. Washington's Tuskegee Institute, emphasizing agricultural education and research for helping African Americans.

At that time, the main cash crop of the South was cotton, which rapidly depleted the soil of nitrates and nutrients. In order to replenish the soil, it was common to plant peanuts because they return nitrates, making the ground productive for the next season of cotton. However, at the time there was no real market for peanuts—so at the end of each season, the peanut harvest was tossed away as garbage. Because of this, farmers went without income from any fields they chose to replenish by growing peanuts rather than planting with cotton. Recognizing this, Dr. Carver determined that if he could find something valuable to do with these peanuts, he could greatly help the sharecroppers.

So, he took a peanut in his hand and prayed a simple prayer: "Great Creator, why did you make the peanut? Why?"[1] Then he set to work, adding a great deal more prayer and meditation along the way. As he described it:

> With such knowledge as I had of chemistry and physics I
> set to work to take the peanut apart. I separated the water,
> the fats, the oils, the gums, the resins, sugars, starches,
> pectoses, pentoses, pentosans, legumen, lysin, the amino,
> and amido acids. There! I had the parts of the peanut all
> spread out before me. Then I merely went on to try different
> combinations of those parts, under different conditions of
> temperature, pressure, and so forth.[2]

In the years to come, George Washington Carver found over 300 uses for the peanut and over 500 products that could be made from things commonly grown on a southern farm. Despite the tremendous value of his discoveries, he only ever took out three patents, following the principle, *"Freely you have received, freely give."*[3] The discoveries he made revolutionized life for the sharecroppers in the South, giving them new sources of income they had previously never imagined from the very things they had right under their noses—from what they had never seen as being of any value. George had delivered them into a new paradigm.

As a man of God and of science, a man of education and of faith, Dr. Carver unlocked mysteries in one of the simplest of God's creations to transform his world. He spent much of his time teaching and preaching wherever the door was open, giving out what advice and instruction he could "for the price of a postage stamp" and teaching others the joy of coming into right relationship with the Creator of the universe.[4] His advice was simple:

> To those who have as yet not learned the secret of true happiness, which is the joy of coming into the closest relationship with the Maker and Preserver of all things: begin now to study the little things in your own door yard [backyard], going from the known to the nearest related unknown, for indeed each new truth brings one nearer to God.[5]

Dr. Carver's worldview not only framed his world, it formed the foundation of his belief that it was a world of unlimited potentialities and possibilities, a world without lids or limitations. His worldview excluded neither God nor science and refused to accept setbacks, prejudices, or unknowns as barriers to what he could accomplish. Whether we live in a mud hut in Africa, a villa in the South of France, a yurt in the Himalayas, a shanty house in the slums of Guatemala, or a chawl in the overpopulated streets of Bombay, we need to open our perspectives and realize a better life is far from impossible if we would but follow Dr. Carver's advice.

Too often we allow our worldviews and perceptions of reality to set limits for us that we don't even realize. We fail to heal ourselves or our living environments because of barriers to change that we accept as the natural order of things, even though they are far from inflexible. These mind-sets are paradigm prisons that can keep entire societies in a state of lack, hunger, illness, conflict, and exploitation. It is what gives way to both beggars and suicide bombers, as well as college professors preaching there is no God and politicians who use their charisma and influence to live luxuriously while those they govern become slowly poorer and more enslaved.

The rich and the influential are not immune to these deceptions either; they are entrapped by similar lies that say that ultimate happiness will come from what they acquire and the personal empires they build—all while they slowly trade little pieces of their souls for things that are of no eternal value.

Yet even Dr. Carver had only part of the story. With the little he had he did great things, but the challenges we face today at the dawn of our new century are no less than what he faced at the dawn of his. We need to open our minds and hearts afresh to what is known and what needs to be revealed. We cannot compromise our potential by just living well enough to be comfortable while building businesses and kingdoms that will one day be nothing more than dust. If we would but simply become who we were created to be, we will change the world around us in ways that will both better it in the short term and mark eternity with marvels beyond what has previously been imagined.

In the very first pages of the Genesis story, God framed the potential of the universe with mysteries—mysteries He takes as much pleasure in revealing as we do in discovering. He locked into everything He created untold solutions for every possible need and desire humanity would ever face. He created mankind with a soul, and He set eternity in our heart, and gave us the ability to respond with courage to any and every impasse—to find solutions to problems and to progress, grow, and prosper in spite of any malevolent force that threatens to annihilate our very existence.[6] He gave humanity the creative genius to rise to every challenge with confidence. He put unlimited potential within each human soul to see and understand—the divine gift of insight.[7] We are endowed with the ability to "see from within" in order to solve problems without. This is our destiny—the only path that leads each individual into a divine sense of purpose, meaning, and hope.

If you look closely at the creation story starting at Genesis 1:1, you will notice something interesting. We are told that on day one, God spoke into the chaos and said, *"Let there be light,"* and on day four, He made the sun and the moon.[8] Is there something wrong here? From where did the light that was *"Let be"* on day one come if not from the sun and the stars?

If we explore the Hebrew word used for *light* on day one, we will discover that it is different from the word used on day four for the *lights* of the sun, moon, and stars. These *lights* (day four word: *mâorah*) would give *light* (day one word: *'owr*) but were not themselves the source of the light (*'owr*) that was created on day one. In fact, if you look at their definitions, they are slightly different. Day one light is light itself, but the lights created on day four were "luminous" objects to give off the light created on day one.[9] As God said, *"let them be lights [mâorah] in the expanse of the heavens to give light ['owr] upon the earth."*[10]

Not only that, but before the creation of the sun and the stars, God had already created vegetation to cover the earth. As we know, it is light, along with water and nutrients from the soil, that gives life to plants, whether that light comes from the sun or a florescent bulb.

I believe this all happens because the light created on day one was much more than the light by which we see. Symbolically, light has long been a metaphor for truth, knowledge, wisdom, revelation, insight, and life. Light is opposed to darkness, which often signifies deception, ignorance, and death. When light enters, darkness flees. Light, therefore, conquers darkness. As it says in Proverbs, *"God delights in concealing things; scientists delight in discovering things."*[11]

Scientists tell us some very interesting things about the property of light. They believe that within light may lie the answers to understanding our universe—namely, what they call a "theory of everything," one that unifies Einstein's theory of relativity, which works for the incredibly huge expanse that is our universe, and quantum mechanics, which is the best theory we have right now for explaining the behavior of matter at the subatomic level. They believe that this is because the speed of light is the defining constant of the universe and is, as far as we know, the upper limit of the speed of matter. As Caltech research scientist Dr. Michelle Thaller puts it, "The speed of light...is the measuring stick of the entire universe."[12]

Light travels at 186,000 miles per second. That means if I stood on the equator and shot a bullet of light from a gun, by the time I released my finger from the trigger the bullet would have already traveled around the earth seven times. In Isaiah 65:24, God tells us, *"Before they call I will answer."* In other words, spiritual things are the only things that can move faster than light.[13]

Thus it must have been, in the beginning, that the spiritual realm had the upper hand in the creation of our universe. Scientists speculate that the nanosecond before the Big Bang, the universe was in fact *"without form and void."*[14] There was nothing, literally nothing—not even space. It is incredibly hard to imagine. If you had been there to watch, even the speck of dust that they say exploded to create the universe would have been too small to see. They believe it was about the size of the nucleus of an atom. Then, suddenly, for some reason— which I believe is that God spoke—there was a tremendous explosion.

As scientists describe it, in a billionth of a billionth of a billionth of a second, the universe went from nothing to everything. Every atom, every gas molecule, every planet, every star, and every galaxy that exists now started forming from the elements that had before been packed into that incredibly small, dense mass. As far as scientists can tell, the universe expanded at least seven billion light years in every direction in that tiniest fraction of a second, making them believe that the universe—which is still expanding—is at least 13.7 billion years old and likely extends several times beyond what we have already discovered. Why do they believe that? Because the light from the farthest things that we can see has taken 13.7 billion years to reach us, and whatever is beyond that we cannot see because the first light of creation from those stars has yet to reach us. What is beyond that? We can only guess. However, scientists believe there must be something, for current estimates of the size of the universe are that it is about 156 billion light years from one edge to the other, with our tiny planet somewhere in its midst.

In that tiniest of a fraction of a nanosecond that was creation, God spoke and the universe simply *was*. I believe that when God said *"Let there be light"* and lit the fuse on the Big Bang, the light He created was not only the light that comes from the sun and the stars, but all of the physical and biological laws that govern the movement of the heavenly bodies and tiniest of electrons, as well as the behavior of cells and every form of life.[15] In that light was all truth, all life, and all potentialities. Mineral, plant, animal, and energy were all defined in that declaration. All that can be known and will ever be known in this material universe was created with that light. God masterfully planned out every minute detail of it. As we are told in Isaiah:

> *Who has measured the waters in the hollow of his hand and marked off the heavens with a span, enclosed the dust of the earth in a measure and weighed the mountains in scales and the hills in a balance?*[16]

The cosmic "dust," if you will, of all matter that was smaller than an atom before the Big Bang became the building blocks of everything that is in the universe today—they were the stem cells of the universe. Imagine the incredible power of creation locked into every subatomic particle emitted at that burst! It would create suns, worlds, galaxies, plants, animals, and eventually you and me! The creative energy and matter that happened when the universe began still lingers *in each of us*. As astrophysicist at the American Museum of Natural History Neil deGrasse Tyson explains:

> Recognize that the very molecules that make up your body—
> the atoms that construct the molecules—are traceable to
> the crucibles that were once the centers of high mass stars
> that exploded their chemically-enriched guts into the galaxy,

enriching pristine gas clouds with their chemistry of life so that we are all connected to each other, biologically; to the earth, chemically; and to the rest of the universe, atomically. That's kind of cool. That makes me smile, and I actually feel quite large.... We are in the universe, and the universe is in us.[17]

Scientists believe that light from the Big Bang permeated the universe about 380,000 years *after* that explosion; however, the first stars did not form until the universe was at least a billion years old. Then our own star, the sun, came into being when the universe was around nine billion years old. How incredibly patient God was in creating a home for us!

Where Genesis 1:1 takes place in this process is a mystery. It could be the instant of the Big Bang, or it could be the day God decided to turn the earth into a living world in a universe He had already set into motion billions of years before, or it could be both, with some kind of gap of several billion years between verses. Or there could be some other explanation. But theories about how long the six days of Genesis really were are too numerous to explore here and are beside the point.

What I want you to see is that when God spoke, the atoms of the universe went forth—called into being from what seems to have been virtual nothingness. Scientists believe that the majority of the most basic elements of the chemical periodic table that exist today—namely hydrogen and helium—were created at this dawning of the universe. In the beginning, every atom that existed was filled with creative power framed by the words of God, and it is still that way today. The elements and life put into them at creation propagate themselves. God created the atoms that formed into molecules that became heavenly bodies that led to life that led to human beings—not necessarily in an evolutionary process as most scientists preach, but certainly by the intelligent design God breathed into them when He spoke the natural universe into being.

Why am I telling you all of this? Because I want you to see that when God designed every rock, plant, creature, gas, and type of energy that exists, there was a mystery locked into each—several mysteries probably—that God knew humanity would one day need to solve in order to discover some new blessing God wanted for His children. And the keys to unlocking these mysteries are buried inside each of us.

Billions of people had lived on the earth and discounted the peanut before George Washington Carver held it in his hand that day and asked God to reveal its mysteries to him. Would he have been able to do that had he discounted his education or been derailed by the pervasive racial prejudice within the South? Probably not. He could have asked, but he would never have had the scientific knowledge to discover all of the uses that he did. What if he had given in to the overwhelming circumstances of being born a slave, being orphaned, and having to work to put himself through school? What if he had not ultimately refused the accolades of the world to take a post of service to his fellow human beings—choosing the solitude of research over the advantages of a titled position? Or what if he had patented every discovery he made and profited off of the poor farmers rather than giving them these things freely so that they could make a better life for themselves? Even with the few patents he did file, he still became wealthy enough to pursue his life's passions without having to worry about how to pay for them. God met His every need as he walked in step with His Spirit. He took a different path, the road less traveled, and as Robert Frost's poem says, that "made all the difference."[18] Carver's real claim to fame was to ask questions that only God could answer. And so it can be with you. You may not have all the answers—or any—but you can ask the God who does.[19]

God's original idea was to create a universe of order and potential in which every creation or creature would add to the overall whole. Human beings were to be a creative partner with God in making it a marvelous place. God was to be our only Lord—not other people, circumstances, or even natural laws. God didn't create leaders and followers—suns and satellites, if you will: those who would be in the center and those who would rotate around them—but a vast plurality of leaders and followers who would exchange places as needed, each stepping into position in the dance of existence, leading and following according to the gifts needed for the circumstance or situation at hand.

Historical religious leaders balked at the idea that the earth was not the center of the universe because in their minds, humanity was the greatest creation that existed, therefore humankind had to be at the center. But God's lesson inscribed in the cosmos was different: "You are not the center of things, but that makes you no less important to Me. I want you to find your place in the dance. I want you to take your place in proper relationship with everything and everyone else, and most importantly I want you to know it all comes through a relationship with Me. I want to show you what I have endued you with. Will you join in the dance with Me?"

What frames your understanding of the world in which you currently live? What paradigms fuel your realities? Where does your inspiration come from? How is your future fashioned? Remember, what we call ordinary today was an extraordinary breakthrough yesterday. Pause to consider what extraordinary breakthrough God wants to reveal to you that can potentially change the way we live tomorrow.

In everything in this universe, including you, there is creative power to change reality—in fact, no matter what we do, we change things for better or worse. We either choose to make things better and plug into the power of the universe for positive, creative change, or we acquiescence to the negative influences of a corrupted world and feed the deterioration and distortion of what is true and beautiful. We have that choice in everything we do. We need to understand that we are creatures without limits. The same "stuff" that God spoke into existence millennia ago and that is still creating and expanding today *is in us*. And in all that, you are just getting the slightest glimpse of the potential God has locked into you. It is time to understand just how to start going from *potential* to *reality*!

Creativity and imagination…is not confined to a small group of leaders. We are at our best when all of the people are encouraged to know that they have great possibilities, and one of their possibilities is to dream. And if they can be encouraged to know that, it is just amazing and beyond our imagination to know what they can imagine.

—Vincent Harding

In a quantum world there are no hidden deeds, and each action by every individual counts. We are here in the world that we create together.

—Gregg Braden, *The Isaiah Effect*

History maker arise…and pursue the potential of your hidden genius!

Reflect on the divinely inspired quote by Dr. Carver, a man of God, science, education, and faith who unlocked the limitless possibilities hidden in the most unassuming of God's creations:

Begin now to study the little things in your own [backyard], going from the known to the nearest related unknown, for indeed each new truth brings one nearer to God.[20]

Dr. Carver understood that a close relationship with the Creator is the only way to access the creativity required to find the kinds of innovative solutions the world needs to thrive in difficult times.

- What is arising in your own backyard that you can take to the nearest related unknown?

Unknowns become knowns when you tap into your God-given genius. Explore the inner workings of your spirit. Where your spirit meets God's Spirit is where you will find the solutions the world needs.

History maker arise...and pray for God's answers to be revealed.

Father, today I come to You seeking Your creative guidance. Show me how I can draw closer to You, to lean in farther than I have before and unearth the riches of Your glory!

Open my heart, eyes, and ears to new ways of knowing, seeing, and hearing from Heaven. Help me unlock the solutions the world needs and reveal the mysteries of Your manifold wisdom—for such a time as this!

Show me, Lord, how to loose the grace, knowledge, and blessings of Heaven into the dark places You have made known to me so I can shine Your light therein. I declare now, "Let there be light!" Amen.

CHAPTER FOUR

who is "i"?

Then I look at my micro-self and wonder,
Why do You bother with us?
Why take a second look our way?
Yet we've so narrowly missed being gods,
bright with Eden's dawn light.

—PSALMS 8:4–5 MSG

All mankind is of one author, and is one volume; when
one man dies, one chapter is not torn out of the book, but
translated into a better language; and every chapter must be
so translated.... No man is an island entire of itself; every
man is a piece of the continent, a part of the main; if a clod
be washed away by the sea, Europe is the less, as well as if a
promontory were, as well as a manor of thy friends or of thine
own were; any man's death diminishes me, because
I am involved in mankind. And therefore never send to
know for whom the bell tolls; it tolls for thee.

—JOHN DONNE, "MEDITATION XVII"

Once the universe was set in motion and an earth was created on
which life and truth could thrive, God introduced into it a partner—
the human being; our forefather, Adam. Removing Adam's rib, God
separated humanity into male and female, creating Eve as a companion
and co-heir to Adam: *"Bone of my bones and flesh of my flesh,"* as Adam
later described her.[1] Man and woman were each individual and unique,
but as they were taken one from the other, they were never truly whole
again without each other. It is a dichotomy we still struggle with
today—the need to be individual, distinctive, and whole on our own,
and yet we can never be totally complete without others. As Donne put
it, "No man [or woman] is an island."[2]

We have the need to be connected, loved, and fully known, and yet
at the same time we need space to look inward, reflect, and sit with our
own souls. We are part of each other to a greater extent than simply
being made up of the same stuff as the universe; we are in each other
more than we are in the universe and the universe is in us—but at the
same time, we are each a universe unto ourselves.

And, oddly enough, the universe needs us to fulfill our potential so
that it can operate at its potential. As Romans 8:19–21 puts it:

> *For the creation waits with eager longing for the revealing*
> *of the sons* [and daughters] *of God. For the creation was*
> *subjected to futility, not willingly, but because of him who*
> *subjected it, in hope that the creation itself will be set free from*
> *its bondage to corruption and obtain the freedom of the glory*
> *of the children of God.*

When humanity lives separately and corruptly, there are ramifications for our planet. While they are often called "acts of God," they
are truly anything but that. Earthquakes, tornadoes, hurricanes, and
the like are not a result of God's divine creation, but of the fall of Adam
and Eve and the sin that continues on the earth. When I use the word
sin, I am not merely speaking of moral failures, but man's failure to
do life with God rather than life separate from Him. However, moral
corruption feeds environmental corruption, sometimes directly in the

sense of pollution and poor stewardship of our natural world and its resources, and sometimes less directly through natural disasters. While some try to make direct connections—e.g., saying that Hurricane Katrina hit New Orleans because it was a sinful city and that the more recent hurricane in Japan struck there because Japan rejected God—I don't think it works that way. Matthew 5:45 tells us, *"For He makes His sun rise on the evil and on the good, and sends rain on the just and on the unjust,"* meaning that when such things happen, they happen indiscriminately.

Hurricane Katrina, the earthquakes in Haiti and Japan, and the destructive tornadoes that tear through Alabama, Georgia, Oklahoma, or anywhere else are not the result of things done in those specific areas; rather, they are the result of the general corruption on the earth through the corruption of human souls. The earth cries out for redemption just as do the souls of mankind. As Romans 8 puts it, the earth is crying out for us to manifest ourselves as the children of God we were created to be. The creative power of righteousness in us affects the very environment around us. Or, as science has found, what we pay attention to changes just by our turning our focus toward it. Or, to paraphrase Chesterton, "Who is responsible for the earthquake in Haiti? *I am.* Therefore, who needs to lend a helping hand to those who were struck by it? *I do.*" Unless individuals act, nothing is going to change.

Thus the place to start in "saving the world" is not necessarily doing some grandiose thing to be counted among the likes of Nelson Mandela, Martin Luther King Jr., Desmond Tutu, Mahatma Gandhi, Susan B. Anthony, or Abraham Lincoln, but becoming the authentic people we were created to be. Men and women like these simply followed their hearts; they did what they felt was right day in and day out, and when that preparation met opportunity, the world became that much more "right" because of their individual impacts.

The power of a single human soul living in the fullness of its unique expression is always underestimated. There is no greater conspiracy than the one of evil contriving to keep you and me from becoming our authentic selves.

Scholars, philosophers, and psychologists have debated at length what exactly is the makeup of a human being. It has long been apparent that human beings have an inner and outer world, a soul on the inside and a physical body on the outside. However, Scripture also tells us that we have a human spirit. As the apostle Paul admonished:

> *Now may the God of peace Himself sanctify you completely, and may your whole **spirit** and **soul** and **body** be kept blameless.*[3]

Likewise, Jesus instructed us:

> *You shall love the Lord your God with all your **heart** and with all your **soul** and with all your **mind** and with all your **strength**.*[4]

And further, the Book of Hebrews points to the fact that while it is difficult to divide what exactly the soul is from what the spirit is, it can be done through spending time in the Word of God:

> *For the word of God is living and active, sharper than any two-edged sword, piercing to the division of **soul** and of **spirit**, of joints and of marrow, and **discerning the thoughts and intentions of the heart**.*[5]

As we see here in Scripture, it is easiest to see us as three parts—the spirit, the soul, and the body. Most commonly, *heart* has in many instances been used synonymously with the human spirit and *mind* with the human soul. In fact, as I have outlined it in other books, the soul houses the mind, will, and emotions of each individual. The Greek word for *soul* is the word ψυχή (*psuche*) that is often Anglicized as "psyche." It is the word from which we get the word *psychology*, or "the study of mind and behavior."[6] Though Bible translators sometimes translate this word as "heart," I believe this refers to the soul as the seat of the emotions, not to be confused with the Greek word for *heart*, which is καρδία (*kardia*), representing the spirit or the *"hidden person of the heart."*[7] As we can see, as we start to dig into this it can quickly become difficult to separate the inner life of the soul from the operations of our human spirits.

As human beings, we straddle two "realities." Almost every religious tradition recognizes that being human means connecting with an inner world and an outer world, the realm of God and the realm of nature, the invisible reality and the visible, the spiritual and the physical. Most recognize the spiritual world as the world that gave birth to our physical world—it is the eternal, while the earth we live on and the universe in which it exists are temporary and secondary in nature. Even psychology has recognized that we have a conscious and an unconscious part of ourselves. Inside we are mind, will, and emotions—only the tip of the iceberg of who we really are and what we are capable of being. Outside, we meet the world with our five senses through a physical body that houses all we are on the inside—it is the vehicle for that which is the "I" of us, our unique and eternal selves that we call our "souls."

The word for *soul* in ancient Greek is the word ψυχή (*psuche*)—which is, as I have already mentioned, the root of the word *psychology*, or the "study of" the *psuche*. The *psuche* is our *personality* in all of its complexity. Essentially, the *psyche* or soul is the inner part of who we are—the part of us that thinks, feels emotions, and makes thousands of decisions every second, many of which we don't even realize we are making because they are so automatic. Within our souls is a part that is conscious—that we are aware of and notice as we run it through our cognitive functions—and another part that is unconscious—the "automatic" part of our selves that influences our actions on the surface through habit and reaction. But deeper down is a sum of all we have ever experienced, hoped for, and desired, and perhaps even things that our parents and ancestors did millennia before, written mysteriously into our genetic code, whether we ever realize it or not. These things color our emotions, which affect our decisions in ways we don't even realize. We meet someone who seems "creepy" and pull away; we are drawn to another; we hear a word or a voice across a crowded room where everyone is talking, and it makes us look to see who spoke.

Science has a hard time recognizing the soul as something separated from the operations of our physical body. Scientists have found that things as ethereal as love, joy, and courage have very real physical manifestations in brain chemistry and electromagnetic pulses. Some have even suggested that perhaps this is all emotions really are—chemical interactions in the brain, whether it be the neurotransmitters released during the birthing and nursing process that attach mothers to children or the adrenaline rush in the heat of a crisis that gives a fireman the extra confidence and strength he needs to save a child from a burning building.

It is interesting to note that when Sigmund Freud—who many consider the father of psychology—looked for a theory of personality, he divided the human being into three parts as well—the ego (from the Greek word for *I*, ἐγώ), the id, and the superego. For Freud, the ego is for all intents and purposes the conscious self, the personality of a person, the place where actions are determined. The ego is "a mediator between...internal needs and the demands of reality."[8] The id is the primal, instinctual part of the person, whose main aim is to fulfill an individual's desire for pleasure, dominated by the drive for *eros* (sexual love) and the death instinct (the human penchant for violence). For Freud, the superego was something that developed in life beyond the power of the ego over the impulses of the id. The superego develops as moral training takes place—the "voice" of the superego being the voice of conscience. This somewhat parallels what we call the soul with Freud's ego, what the Bible calls "flesh" with the id, and the spirit with the superego. While in some ways these are forced comparisons, they are still worth noting.

So, if we were to draw a picture of ourselves as three parts, you could think of it in a couple of different ways. First, you could visualize us as three concentric circles, one inside the other, with the spirit at the center, surrounded by the soul, housed within the body (see Diagram A). Beyond the body (outside of the outer circle) is the physical world; through the soul and "within" the spirit is the spiritual world. If you can visualize it, think of the soul as the center of a wormhole between two universes, one being the physical realm, the other the spiritual. We interact with the spiritual through our spirits in the same way that we interact with the physical through our bodies.

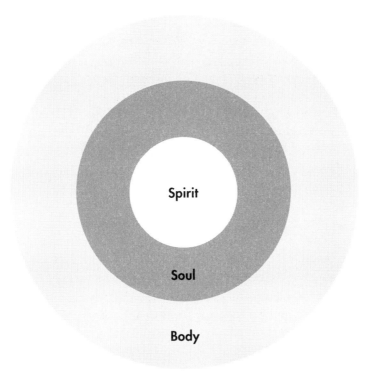

Diagram A

Another way to look at it would be to think of our makeup as three parts of a pie (see Diagram B), with a line dividing the body from the spirit and the soul straddling that line. In this representation, you would need to think of there being a solid line between the spirit and body, but a dotted line through the soul—which is in contact with both the spirit and the body.

A third way to look at this might be in the form of a square with three different "layers," like Neapolitan ice cream (see Diagram C). In this diagram, we again see that the spirit must communicate with the body through the soul, as well as vice versa. You might also imagine it as being more like a rainbow than having strict divisions between each part—as if the spirit blends into the soul and then into the body rather than each being completely distinct.

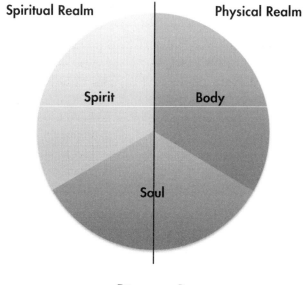

Diagram B

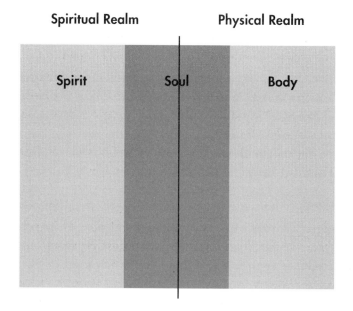

Diagram C

For example, we say that the mind is part of the soul, but it also has a physical manifestation in the brain. What happens in the brain affects the mind, and what happens in the mind physically changes the brain. As things are considered in the soul—when we choose the thoughts we will think—the brain responds in how it fires electrical impulses and releases chemicals that form memories, restructure neural pathways, and create attitudes and behavioral patterns. (We will talk further about this when we look more closely at the mind and what scientists are discovering about the brain in the next chapter.)

The first thing I want you to see in these diagrams is that for each of us, the soul is the mediator between the spiritual and the physical—between the spirit and the body. If the mind, will, and emotions are in our soul, it is through our spirit and physiology that we take in pertinent information so that our souls can interpret those "sensings" and make decisions. In this way, our wills are not so much what we associate with "willpower"—which is the strength to consistently choose according to a set of principles over immediate impulses and desires—but a split-second "decider" and "decision maker." Our will is like an on-and-off switch—it decides either yes or no. According to it, we either do something or we don't; we either accept thoughts and opinions as part of our worldview or we reject them. It determines whether we act on something now, wait, or never act at all.

It is this power to decide—our "free will"—that is the starting place of healing our souls, finding and living as our authentic selves, and reaching out to affect the world around us.

I like to think of "Will" as a little "mini-me" deep inside, sitting in a sophisticated, state-of-the-art control center, taking in information from all kinds of different places, with a board of switches and knobs sitting before it (something like the control room in the animated movie *Inside Out*). At this little self's fingertips are readings from our emotions, thoughts, input from the five senses, memories, and the conscience, which is the voice of the human spirit. If God speaks to "Will," it is through the spirit, because the spirit is connected to the spiritual world and is the conduit through which it interacts with spiritual things. Once Will has taken all of these things in and made its analysis, it makes a yes or no decision.

The problem is that, for most of us, Will is asleep at the wheel. Rather than embracing that power for decision-making in our lives, we sleepwalk through life, not allowing Will to act independently of the habits we have formed over the years. When our spouse speaks to us and it triggers some ancient memory of how we related with a sibling or parent, we react the same way to them as we did when that memory was triggered at other times in the past. We never grow up and take responsibility for our words or actions. When we face food choices as an adult, we make the same choices we developed as children growing up, even though our metabolism is now very different and has different needs. When we face challenges in work or life, we tend to react to them exactly the same way we did in elementary school, either embracing the challenge to succeed or falling back on being the person our third grade teacher thought we were—good or bad.

If we are to heal our souls, we have to wake Will up and take back the power to control our decisions from the habits and patterns of our pasts. While it is as simple as this to explain, it is not nearly so simple to do. We have years and years behind us of making bad decisions and falling into behavior patterns that we perform without conscious thought. It took time to develop these bad habits, and likewise, it will take some time to right them. The good news is, however, that new habits only really take about 21 to 30 days to form. Brain science is showing today that our minds are much more pliable than we thought in previous decades. When we start to think in new ways and practice new decision patterns, our brains respond by rewiring themselves to create different patterns of behavior, and the more we practice these patterns the more we let go of the old.

Dr. Vilayanur S. Ramachandran, called the "Marco Polo of neuro-science," made the following observation: "There are 100 billion neurons in the adult human brain and each neuron makes 1,000 to 10,000 contacts with other neurons in the brain. The number of permutations and combinations of brain activity exceeds the number of elementary particles in the universe."[9] Further, modern science has discovered that the unconscious mind performs about 400 billion actions a second—from controlling our heartbeat and breathing to seeing things out of the corner of our eye and determining whether they are worthy of our attention or can be safely ignored—while the conscious mind processes only about 2,000 bits of information a second. Because of this, many of us fall prey to bad habits of which we are not even aware.

Like I said, Will is asleep at the wheel or, more likely, distracted by watching too much television, listening to music with lyrics that contradict our values, or obsessing with relationship issues in all the wrong ways. We are constantly bombarded with messages trying to get us to make others wealthier and more popular—all while a sleepwalking herd of humanity follows those dictates with little conscious realization that it is doing them no good. The truth is that whatever we invest our attention in profits (if you don't believe me, look at television, professional sports, and video games as examples—the more people focus their attention on such things, the more valuable they become and the more money they generate for their creators). What we pay attention to channels where all we have that is valuable goes—namely our time, our talents, and our treasure.

The first step in the healing process is to wake our souls up and begin to recognize the patterns in our lives. We must get Will back to work making decisions according to consciously chosen principles rather than the unconscious patterns fed to us from our culture that exploit us for the profit of others. Scripture warns us that there is a way of the world and a way of God: *"You were dead...following the course of this world...carrying out the desires of the body and the mind, and were by nature children of wrath, like the rest of mankind."*[10]

The way of the world leads to death, but the way of God leads to a more abundant life. Which do you choose? For the truth is, unless we wake up and decide, we are just puppets sleepwalking through life, giving our wealth and substance to those least likely to use it for anything but selfish reasons.

God has a different plan:

*For I know the plans I have for you, declares the Lord, plans
for welfare and not for evil, to give you a future and a hope.*[11]

And:

I [Jesus] *came that they may have life and have it
abundantly.*[12]

Before we talk more about this, we need to take a closer look at
the mind, will, and emotions in light of what science has been learning
about them in recent years. This will help us understand how God
originally wired us for this abundant life—and how to align ourselves
with His truths so we can start changing our world for the better.

*Our deepest calling is to grow into our own authentic
selfhood, whether or not it conforms to some image
of who we ought to be. As we do so, we will not only find
the joy that every human being seeks—we will also find
our path of authentic service in the world.*

—PARKER PALMER, *LET YOUR LIFE SPEAK*

*To claim to live at the center of the world is clearly a
delusional statement from the standpoint of the separate
self, but from the perspective of your essential being,
it is only stating a truth latent in every awakening soul;
the core truth of our consciousness* [is] *that our awareness,
moving as our thoughts, desires, feelings, and senses,
generates an experiential reality or world around us.
We are the authors of this world.*

—DEEPAK CHOPRA AND OPRAH WINFREY,
CREATING PEACE FROM THE INSIDE OUT

The human heart is the first home of democracy.
It is where we embrace our questions.
Can we be equitable? Can we be generous?
Can we listen with our whole beings, not just our minds,
and offer our attention rather than our opinions?
And do we have enough resolve in our hearts to act
courageously, relentlessly, without giving up—ever—
trusting our fellow citizens to join with us
in our determined pursuit?

—TERRY TEMPEST WILLIAMS, "ENGAGEMENT"

History maker arise...and become the "I" who can change the world!

Ripples of hope can be felt and absorbed only if each distinct individual connects with others who bring their own cadre of diverse talents, mental acuities, and even idiosyncrasies to the whole body. Your "I" value is so vital to adding to the world commodity that allowing it to diminish or fade in any way prohibits the fullness of abundant life that Christ came to offer.

Choosing to embrace the "I" of today and shed the "you" of yesteryears will advance the manifestation of yourself as a child of God, releasing the creative power of righteousness that affects the physical and spiritual environment around you.

Determine today what unhealthy habits and detrimental reactions, born in the past and nourished through the years, must be dealt with—replacing each with healthy habits, honorable attitudes, and respectful reactions to other "I's" who make up the whole of you. If need be, write the changes you want to make and tick off each one, day after day, until they become second nature.

History maker arise...and pray for God's help to live more authentically and congruently.

As you come before your Creator to pray, imagine His beautifully blended and exquisitely colored rainbow arch in the sky—communicating His promise of life and hope to humankind. Likewise, your spirit communicates with your body through your soul, blending your spirit, soul, and body with God's omnipotence to form a kaleidoscope of beauty within you.

Father God, bring focus to the "I" of me so I can develop fully as an integral part of Your worldwide family. May my inner and outer selves reflect the authentic me who can unite with others to create ripples powerful enough to wash over the world with righteousness and selfless acts of compassion and mercy. Amen.

PART TWO

DRIVING CURRENTS
OF CHANGE

The heart is the last frontier…. "Changing your heart"
is a synonym for overcoming unconscious bias. …It's becoming
more conscious about what's going on inside us and then working
with that. This moment we're in is not just a social crisis and not
just a political crisis. It's a spiritual crisis.

—ISABEL WILKERSON, "THE HEART IS THE LAST FRONTIER"

CHAPTER FIVE

wired for actualization

The world that you want to transform in a just manner will not be transformed because you yourselves are not transformed. And also, so long as you refuse to change yourselves, the world will not change. But the world can change if you change. How do you change? By listening to God, because as the sun is always shining, so God is constantly speaking.

—Auguste Gratry

I want you to know that you are not wired for failure; you are wired for success and fulfillment. If you don't believe me, then let's take some time to look at the human brain and what it tells us about our minds and souls. The latest discoveries in brain research are truly amazing. So much of what we understood about the brain before the 21st century was simply based on assumptions made on shallow research. Scientists first believed that once your brain was fully formed, that was pretty much it. While the brain learned and experienced things after growing to full size—the brain is about 95 percent of its full

size by age 7 and slowly continues to grow to full size until around
the age of 21—they believed it really didn't change much after that.
For decades, child psychologists taught that the first five years of life
indelibly established who we would become. The traumas or love we
experienced or didn't experience in those years defined the foundation
of our personalities, and once we grew into adolescence, the patterns of
our lives were pretty much set in stone.

The most startling thing found by advances in our ability to
scan the brain and watch how it operates is that brain development
is not so much about size, but about interconnectedness. While the
brain is nearly full size at age 7, it also has an incredible number
of connections at that age—roughly a billion. This number is truly
overwhelming for the conscious mind, which is probably why kids
can seem a little goofy at that age—they are open to learning so
much that it is hard to choose to act correctly. As the child grows
into the initial years of adolescence, around age 11, the brain starts
to massively rewire itself for efficiency. Unused connections are
sacrificed for creating "superhighways" of the most used connections.
This can be summed up in what is called Hebb's axiom: *neurons that
fire together wire together.* In other words, once we take a particular
course of thought or emotion, we create a pattern; once a pattern is
established, given similar circumstances, we are more likely to follow
that pattern again than we are to randomly follow a different course
unless our conscious will chooses a different path. Life and thought
patterns that are repeatedly followed grow from virgin wilderness to
footpaths to trails to roads to freeways.

A child who experiences a recurring negative attitude from a
parent will begin to translate that stimulus into negative thoughts
about himself or herself—the more it happens, the faster and more
subconsciously it happens as well. Thus, children—who are not yet
mature enough to recognize that the actions of others might not be
in response to them personally—will think a mother or father who is
angry because of work is angry with them. At this age, the ego, or "I,"
within is the center of everything; therefore, everything that happens
outside of us *must* be about us. Eventually, that will create a negative

self-image if most of the input from around us is negative. By the time this little "I" is dating, he or she will respond to an angry look or remark with the thought, *I'm a worthless human being*, because that is what was formed in them when their parents continually got angry. These neural pathways from seeing anger to experiencing feelings of shame and negative self-image have fired together so often that they have gone from a rabbit trail to a bullet train, none of it conscious. This pattern is why family therapists and marriage counselors estimate that roughly 80 percent of emotional conflict between couples is based on events that happened long before they ever met. Remember that only five ten-millionths of a percent of the things the brain is doing are actually evaluated by the conscious mind; that means many of the patterns we follow are completely without conscious thought.

However, here is good news: once we bring those patterns into the conscious mind, we can, through the will, decide to start a different pathway that, over time and repeated conscious choice, will create a different superhighway that leads to a more positive self-image. And while the first negative pattern took years to develop, researchers tell us it takes roughly 30 days to imbed a new one. That means if we consciously think about something for five to ten minutes a day every day for 30 days, we will form a new mental pattern strong enough to unconsciously change our reactions to a given stimuli. The learning of something new—the revelation of a new truth or the acceptance of a new principle—has the power to literally *change our minds*.[1]

Furthermore, the brain doesn't have different polar opposite chemicals for different polar opposite emotions. In other words, the brain is not wired for good *and* evil, if you will, but only good *and* the absence of good. The brain recognizes only normal functioning versus abnormal functioning—or you might say, contentment or crisis, calm or stress. So a happy, properly functioning brain is not operating on one set of chemicals while the panic-stricken brain is operating on another set of chemicals, but the contented brain is functioning on the right amount of chemicals while the brain in crisis is operating on an imbalance or lack of those same chemicals. In this light, there is not good and evil going on in the brain based on the influence of different biochemicals, but there is right and wrong taking place because there are either the right amounts of certain chemicals or the wrong amounts of those same chemicals. And again, the power of will—the power of choice—can help change these patterns. This is why depression and other mental ailments can be treated with medications—those medications work to return biochemical levels to "normal" and thus help the person begin to choose new patterns for how they respond to negative circumstances because their brains are now functioning properly.

Extreme trauma or abuse—especially when we are young— will disintegrate memories and emotional patterns, disrupting and blocking out things too painful to remember. As human beings, our strongest negative emotion is shame, and our unconscious mind will do almost anything to avoid experiencing it. This can have very negative effects on intimacy and relationships in general. When the subconscious mind disconnects because a pattern has been triggered due to the shame about a memory we have repressed, there may be no way to re-establish a healthy connection other than with the help of a professional counselor or psychologist.

Because of the power of choice, siblings born in the same household and who live through the same circumstances can still have different reactions to the same stimuli. Take for example two children who grow up in a home where the mother has gone to prison. One of the kids might look at that and say, "Man, life is unfair. This world is too awful to live in. I think I will do drugs and check out," while the other will think, "My mom made some bad choices. I am going to go to school, study hard, and become a psychiatrist so that I can help people learn how to avoid making those same mistakes."

Hear what I am saying: *circumstances do not control your life!* Circumstances come, and circumstances go. But it is not the circumstances we face that decide our paths; it is our reaction to them. It is our thoughts and decisions in response to those circumstances that make the difference between those who overcome and those who are overcome. So many are stuck in a victim mentality, wondering why bad things happen to good people, but I am telling you we need to change that pattern. Instead, we need to have the attitude of a good person who is ready to happen to bad things!

We are not wired to be defeated; we are wired for joy and fulfillment—we are wired to self-actualize!

While we are creatures of two realms—part of us in the unseen realm of the spirit and part of us in the physical world—it is not so easy to separate the one part of us from the other. Every action of the mind (the "unseen" thought life) has a counterpart reaction in the physical brain. The original design and intent of this is quite remarkable. If we had to consciously take in and react to every stimulus that comes to us as we grow up and learn, it would soon be overwhelming, and we would never get anywhere. In essence, we would continually be learning the same lessons over and over again without ever retaining what we are learning.

Take, as an example, learning your multiplication tables. When I was first introduced to the concept of multiplication, it wasn't easy for me to understand, but I applied myself. I did the tables, I took time tests, and I developed neural memory pathways that reacted faster and faster. At first, I would see something like 6 × 7, and I would have to calculate it out, taking a few seconds to count by sevens and use my fingers until I got to 42. However, after months of repetition, I got to where I would see 6 × 7 and immediately 42 would pop into my mind. Because of this, when I went on to algebra I could focus on learning new, more difficult concepts because I didn't have to take up space in my conscious mind to reason out every basic multiplication problem when I saw it—those would come automatically because I had memorized them, and that gave me the chance to learn something new.

Thus it was God's design that we would learn and experience things and get smarter and more capable every year we live. Did you know that the human brain has the capability of collecting and archiving three million years' worth of memories and information? What an incredible ability! Imagine all the wisdom and knowledge God intended for us to have! Imagine, if you simply chose to apply yourself, how many abilities and how much knowledge you could acquire! Instead, unfortunately, most of us fill our heads with the same old junk year after year—and end up getting the same old results year after year—then wonder why things don't get any better!

Of course, when God engineered our ancestors Adam and Eve with these capabilities and put them on the earth to thrive, human beings were designed to know only good. Before he knew about evil, Adam was able to meet every animal on earth, give it a name, and then remember that name![2] And thus the problem—just as the mind has a cumulative ability to learn good things and compound ability upon ability when things are going well, it also has the capacity to accumulate hurtful, image-shattering, and harmful thoughts and memories and let their effects compound.

Now perhaps you can more easily see why our belief paradigms either aid or hinder our growth as human beings. Right attitudes—confidence tempered by humility, ambition tempered by care for others, and so forth—drive us toward maximizing our potential, while wrong attitudes—jealousy, low self-esteem, greed, lust, and so forth—put one obstacle after another between us and our dreams. So much of this happens in the unconscious patterns we allow to form in our attitudes and demeanor toward others that we can virtually sleepwalk through life without a clue as to why things are going wrong.

To better understand this, let's take a deeper look at how God designed our brains as a tool for our minds, wills, and emotions to help shape the course of our lives.

The brain is a multifaceted "supercomputer" of an organ, and it can be divided in different ways. Two of the most informative ways are, first, to look at it from its most basic functions from the bottom up and, second, to look at its left and right halves, or hemispheres, that each process information differently.

From the bottom up, the brain has three basic divisions: 1) the R-complex, 2) the limbic circuitry, and 3) the neocortex. The R-complex is made up of the brain stem, which connects to the spinal cord, and the cerebellum. The brain stem controls basic functions like heartbeat, breathing, and blood pressure. The cerebellum is sort of like an internal gyroscope that helps maintain our sense of balance, and more recent research suggests that it is also involved in our sense of emotional stability. This part of the mind operates almost completely unconsciously, though if we involve our conscience minds we can affect it, like when you hold your breath or relax your body.

On the other hand, this part has a direct hotline to our stress and "fight-or-flight" responses. When we touch something hot, there is an immediate reaction. We don't have to stop and consider, "Wow, there is something stimulating pain at the end of my fingertips! Oh no, look! That burner my finger is touching is on! And there is smoke rising from my flesh! I had better pull my hand away!" Instead, without a conscious thought, it takes a split microsecond from the sensation of pain to your hand pulling itself away. You will also notice your heart racing a little faster as your system gets a shot of adrenaline. At the same time, your immune system is already on alert to start healing your burn, sending antibodies to the affected area even as you walk to the sink to put it under running water.

The second part of the brain is the limbic circuitry. This has also been called the paleomammalian brain. This network of neuron tracts and clusters of neuron cells is largely responsible for recognizing and remembering fear, noticing environmental changes, both internally and outside of our bodies, and experiencing and remembering pleasure. In some ways, you could think of it as the home of Freud's id. This "middle" portion of the brain then feeds these primal emotions into the cortex, where they are further defined as the full spectrum of emotions that human beings can experience—joy, distrust, disgust, pride, anger, hurt, confidence, admiration, shame, and so forth. All of this happens rather unconsciously again—sort of like how you can't be happy and notice yourself being happy in the same instant. The first is the output of the limbic circuitry creating an emotion; the second is the work of the cortex trying to define it. This is not absolute, of course, as we can go back and forth several times within the blink of an eye, but again, this part of the mind creates emotions that affect us without a conscious thought pattern getting involved in the process.

The third part of the brain is the neocortex or the neomammalian brain. This, as you might guess from the names of the different parts, is what sets us apart from animals as the most intelligent of creatures on the earth. This part of the brain is home to our cognitive/linguistic, higher social, abstract, creative, and motor skills abilities. The part of the brain that really sets us apart as intelligent beings is called the prefrontal cortex. This is where love is recognized, where we mull over and interpret things that have happened to us, things that we have seen in a movie, or things that we wonder about in a painting that inspires us—where we make the leap from learning the multiplication tables to algebra. The prefrontal cortex houses the control center of the brain where that little "mini-me" sits in the command center that is the will. This is the part of the brain that takes care of the 2,000 or so deliberate actions, thoughts, or decisions we make each second that are conscious activity; the rest run in the wondrous unconscious mind, keeping everything humming so that the conscious mind can create, be entertained, study, or whatever it is we are using it for at the moment. It is the place where we decided what to believe or not believe, make choices that form our paradigms, and basically have control over the things that make us individual and unique in the vast ocean of humanity, with all its myriad possibilities.

The other way to look at the brain is to recognize that its left and right halves take care of different ways of interpreting the world, and we can sort of "live" with an emphasis on one side or the other, causing "imbalances" in how we perceive the way things really are. A communication line called the corpus callosum connects these two hemispheres. Researchers tell us that the left side of the brain (which controls the right side of our bodies and is generally dominant for right-handed people) is responsible for language, logical, linear, and literal processing. It is the part of the brain with which we categorize, label, order, and make sense of the world. This part of the brain is more black and white—like a light switch, it likes to see things as either on or off, right or wrong, without any gray areas in between. This part of our brain doesn't like ambiguities and loves to make a story of everything so that we can make sense of what we experience—even if, sometimes, the connections we piece together to make the story have no basis in fact. This part of our brain so longs to put a pattern to things that it will even do so to our own harm.

An example would be that as children, we might make an association between our father's furrowed brow and the anger he expresses when his brow arched in that way. Being children, with self-centered and limited understandings of the world, we might interpret Dad's anger to mean we caused that anger and, therefore, are bad people. All this gets jumbled together in our minds, and again, much of it happens unconsciously. But the more we see Dad's furrowed brow and experience him being upset, the more that pattern is "fired together" to make an instant response without us even realizing it. Then, years later, we get engaged to a wonderful person, and in planning for the wedding our spouse-to-be furrows their brow. Internally, the superhighway pattern of our childhood story kicks in—our fiancé is angry, we are the cause, and we are horrible, awful people for making them angry. Of course, they may have furrowed their brow because they were weighing the options between different kinds of flowers or different patterns for china, but our old story pattern kicks in regardless of what is really going on. Taken to an extreme, this pattern could lead us to break off the engagement, making ridiculous excuses about how we don't deserve to be married or some such thing, all because we interpret things according to preconceived perceptions—not realizing our reactions have no actual basis in reality. Our wrong perspectives can lead to harmful actions.

The right brain, on the other hand, loves abstractions, creative thinking, and taking in experiences as a whole without needing to break them apart and give names to each piece. The right hemisphere loves rainbows and defies black-and-white evaluations as over-simplistic and narrow-minded. This part of our brain allows us to see things as three-dimensional and to recognize relationships between the objects in that space. It is the nonverbal side of our brain that recognizes the 60 to 90 percent of communication that comes in body language, gestures, expressions—those things that communicate without words. This is the big picture side of us, whereas the left often has trouble seeing the forest because there are so many trees. It is this part of our brain that helps us realize if a friend is down, even when they say everything is fine.

The left side is drawn to rules and standards, the right side to the uniqueness of each different set of circumstances; and in many ways, the latter prefers the exception to the rule. The left side is good at defining and evaluating options, the right side at coming up with options that are "out of the box." Our left side has a tendency to be somewhat conservative; our right side, without constraint, can become flamingly liberal.

Working together, these two hemispheres really do marvelous things. Through proper training, they can look at something and recognize if it is real or not in a split second, even though other experts have been working painstakingly for months to determine its authenticity and come to no conclusion (an ability discussed in Malcolm Gladwell's *Blink*).[3] Our brains can look at a beautiful painting, appreciate it, and then begin putting into words why it is so incredible. Or we can experience God in His majesty and then find ways to communicate that to others who have yet to know Him in any personal way. Dominated too much by one side or the other, the imbalance can put us at cross-purposes with our own God-given destinies.

I think it is interesting to note that these two functions of the brain (the on-or-off left brain and the spectral, holistic right brain) are reflective of the properties of light, which scientists see as both particles and waves. Particles exist in a stream—resembling a dotted line with "on" and "off" segments—while waves are continuous oscillations that vary in intensity, vibration, or degree but are a whole from one end to the other. If both are needed in our brains to grasp truths, then is that because the truths that were released as light on the first day of creation have a similar nature? We need both black-and-white and rainbow-spectrum thinking to understand them.

Imbalances in brain function can cause normally "good" processes to become corrupted and stressed, turning the analysis of a set of any circumstances into warped or "toxic" thinking. When we become too dogmatic (left-brained) or too accepting of everything (right-brained), we can create behavior patterns that squelch our potential and poison our relationships. Add substance abuse or addictions, prejudice and racism, poverty and hunger, or maniacal hatred and access to weapons to this process, and all hell can break loose. It can simply be "stinking thinking" that makes people constantly fight with anyone in authority or create rivalries that erupt in continual conflict and acts of violence, as we see in the Middle East or parts of Africa—tribalism becomes extreme and turns to war. In some ways, it is so easy to understand what needs to change in us as individuals, but in others it is so complicated to fix because there are so many layers to it. In one respect, it is simply about changing people's minds. On the other hand, how do you change the mind-set of an entire nationality or ethnic group?

Oddly enough, though, such remarkable changes do happen. The Christian term *revival* has been used to mark times of great expansion of the Christian faith, but there is really much more to it. Also called times of "awakening"—which fits well with the sleepwalking metaphor we used earlier—it was more about cultural change than recruiting new church members. In periods of great revival and renewal, people took on the principles of love, forgiveness, giving, and helping others and put away corrupting activities in order to transform their cultures. People's hearts were knit together to take on causes of social reform in order to change their societies. They worked together to build homes for each other, gathered together regularly to pray over each other's concerns, and made meals for each other when they were facing tough times. Communities thrived, commerce thrived, and inventiveness thrived.

We need such spiritual revolutions today to free people, turn the tides of hatred, and lift up the well-being of each and every human being on the planet. This type of revolution doesn't come from conflict but from cooperation. When there was class unrest in the 1700s in England and France, France had a revolution that became a bloodbath while England experienced the Great Awakening that revitalized every aspect of society and community. War has always been a win-lose proposition, but awakening is always win-win. While this doesn't mean there isn't evil in the world that needs to be opposed, I am a great believer in taking the battle to the spiritual realm and seeking victory through prayer rather than taking the fight to the streets with bombs and AK-47s.

However, if our prayers are to carry the power needed to overcome the deep conflicts and enormous challenges facing our world, then we'll first need to win the battles raging in our souls. We'll need to institute peace within our interior lives if we are to advocate for peace before the departments and agencies of our nations. When that peace reigns within—peace that transcends understanding—only then will we walk in the authority and power necessary to overcome the barriers that continually oppose it.[4] There are spiritual forces working to oppose your peace, and therefore your authority and power, but you are in possession of a weapon greater than any of those forces—the love of God.[5]

Don't underestimate the power of God's love at work in your heart. According to author Gregg Braden, what stirs our hearts creates magnetic waves that not only influence our physical health, but also create currents that travel through the atmosphere for miles beyond our physical location. When we have a feeling in our hearts, we're creating electric and magnetic waves inside of our bodies that extend beyond our bodies into the world around us.

Research shows that those waves extend not just one meter or two meters, but many kilometers beyond where our heart physically resides. That's how we influence the physical world around us—we can literally rearrange the atoms of physical matter through these fields if we learn to focus and hone this language.[6]

Love, after all, is contagious, but if we are going to spread it, we must let it have its way within us first. We must let it come into each and every decision we make. We must recognize the toxic thought and behavior patterns of our lives and replace them with healthy ones. As we do that, we will become world changers, and then, when we plug into the creativity of Heaven, the power for cultural transformation will know no limits.

Think of love...as a way of being and a way of living that opens us to our fullness and to our best possibilities.

—Vincent Harding

Unconditional love...surrounds us with a charged force field that makes us want to grow from the inside out— a force field that is safe enough to take the risks and endure the failures that growth requires.

—Parker Palmer, *A Hidden Wholeness*

History maker arise...to a self-actualization awakening!

Christ was recorded as saying, *"Hypocrite! First get rid of the log in your own eye; then you will see well enough to deal with the speck in your friend's eye."*[7] Michael Jackson sang about starting with the man in the mirror and having him change his ways; "if you want to make the world a better place, take a look at yourself, and then make a change!"[8]

Taking steps to discover who you really are can be daunting, even frightening. The road to awakening yourself to your self begins with first knowing and believing that God loves you as you are, as you were, and as you will be. His unconditional love should encourage and motivate you to step out in faith—to awaken the glorious you longing to emerge. The world is waiting for you to make that change!

History maker arise...and pray for a new depth of love.

You, Lord God, are the ultimate foundation of every person's spirit, soul, and body. To become a significant vessel to drive the currents of change for the betterment of Your Kingdom and our world, I commit to crushing the incompatible patterns in my life that were unfortunately set in stone during my youth.

Forgive me, Father, for not accepting people as they are and trying to mold them into my inauthentic self. Revive and renew within me Your love, forgiveness, and self-sacrifice, that I might become an instigator of social and cultural transformation in societies lacking justice and righteousness. Amen.

CHAPTER SIX

point of decision, point of power

If we all did the things we were capable of doing,
we would literally astound ourselves.

—Thomas Edison

While a great deal of what happens in our brain happens without a conscious thought, the other side of the coin is that what we set our mind on affects the course of our lives. Our mind operates both collaboratively and independently of the brain. Unless we are deliberate about how we think, we will go through life unaware of the incredible potential we possess both physiologically and spiritually—as if we were the living dead, sleepwalking through life.

This is why the Scriptures say, *"Awake, you who sleep, arise from the dead, and Christ will give you light."*[1] When we sleepwalk through life, we are people of little hope—cultural automatons who don't realize we are products of environments over which we actually have control, mindlessly driven by only our most basic needs, desires, and responses to cultural stimuli. We might say, "Wow! This is really living!" Yet there is no life in living primarily to *"feed our appetites,"* trapped by our own desires, all while *"our souls go hungry."*[2]

An authentic life is an honest, empowered life that not only gives us self-awareness, but also makes us aware of the needs of others. It is a life that allows us to confront the issues in our own characters by being transparent and perhaps letting some of our skeletons out of the closet.

At the same time, it's not only about identifying your shortcomings and trying to extinguish them. You cannot pluck established patterns out of your life. Habits don't die because you sit around saying, "I'm not going to do that anymore. I'm not going to do that anymore. I'm not going to do that anymore." You cannot extinguish a bad habit by resisting it; you have to replace it with a habit that is good.

Every time you come to a point of decision—particularly an impasse in your life where you feel stuck, bored, or aren't sure which road to take—there are really only three options. You can conform, quit, or create.

Let's take those multiplication tables again as an example. Let's say you are in third grade and your class is working through some worksheets as your teacher goes from desk to desk answering questions. You feel bored. You feel like your head hurts from looking at all those numbers. As this happens, you have only three options for what you can do.

First, you can conform. You look around the room to see what other people are doing. Since most of the people are working quietly, you decide to do that same thing. You go through the motions of filling out your sheet. You don't really care if the answers are right or wrong; you are just trying to live out your "sentence" until you get that "get out of jail" card called the recess bell. You don't double-check your answers. You don't invest much of yourself in what you are doing. You are just sleepwalking through the assignment, going with the flow, doing what you see everyone else doing, conforming to the norm.

The second option you have is to quit. Instead of doing your work-sheet, you pull out a slip of paper and start writing a note to your friend sitting three chairs behind you. You draw or scribble on your paper, turning the 9s into little faces and the 7s into sailboats. Or maybe you start acting up and throwing things at another friend who sits a couple of chairs over. You might even raise your hand and start whining. "Mrs. Brown, why do we have to do this? It's too hard. Can't you read us a story or something? Can I go to the bathroom?" These are just a few examples of what you might do, but essentially you have quit. Whatever it was you were supposed to be using your time for is the last thing on earth you are going to do. You would rather sit and stare at the ceiling than get anything out of your math time that day.

Or, you could take the third option and be a creator. You're bored out of your gourd so you decide to make what you are doing more fun. You pull another sheet of paper out of your desk and make a box on it, write the numbers down the side and across the top, and start timing yourself to see how quickly you can fill it out. You pull out some index cards and make your own flash cards. Because both you and one of your friends have finished the worksheet, you ask if you can go sit in the carpeted area of the room and challenge each other on how fast you can get through all of the flashcards. Or maybe you create a multiplication table game you can play by yourself or with others. You are a problem solver, and you are not going to waste even one minute of your own valuable time. When the recess bell finally rings, you are surprised that the time went by so fast, and you are almost disappointed to have to leave your game. Faced with a challenge, you found a creative way to find a solution that was your own, and because of that you learned something and helped other people get through that difficult time as well.

When we bring things into our conscious minds, we have a chance to sit back and interpret what we are seeing and decide on a course forward. Each time we choose a particular course, we strengthen that pathway in our brains, making it more likely we will choose that path again in the future. Whatever we pay attention to, laying a pattern in our brains, becomes stronger. Our choices change the course of our lives, even if it is just one small course correction at a time.

Naturally, when we are born it is not like we come into the world making a lot of conscious choices. For the most part, we are a blank slate, and from the moment we first see our mother's face in the delivery room we start learning. Our five senses have had little to take in until then.

Now suddenly, the world is full of wonders. We start to associate the face we are now seeing with the voice we heard while we were in the womb. Everything is a wonder of light and dark splotches, and it will take us months to be able to learn the difference between a chair and a plant. We don't really begin understanding three-dimensional space until we start crawling around and learning there is distance from one object to the next. We discover that cats are soft and their claws are sharp. We learn some things are pleasant and others are painful. We learn language, how to read facial expressions, and millions of other things we are exposed to or need for survival. As Curt Thompson puts it in his book *The Anatomy of the Soul*, "Parents who provide for their children's physical and emotional security free the brains of their infants, toddlers, and adolescents to wander off in the direction of Tinkertoys, baseball, and Tschaikovsky."[3] Bit by bit we learn the nature of the physical world into which we have emerged.

As far as our little minds are concerned, at this point it is all about us. Everything that happens is related directly to the little "me" that everyone coos at and cuddles. It is how the foundation of our self-image is created as we learn about and react to the world. However, the downside of this is that if Mom and Dad are always fighting, then that is all about us as well. We see ourselves as the cause of any and every conflict. We weren't designed to live in a constant emergency mode with stress and anger all the time so our minds compensate by distorting memories or creating coping behaviors.

So, depending on the early environment we experience, we learn that the world is either a safe, loving, the-possibilities-are-limitless type of place, or we learn that the world is full of danger, conflict, and lack. This is why the word *parent* is a verb as well as a noun—it's a tough job that takes dedicated and conscientious action.

Now this may raise into your mind the question of nature versus nurture—does our personality develop because of our genetic makeup and its myriad possibilities for personality, or are we more influenced by the environment in which we are raised? While this has long been debated by researchers, recent findings point to the fact that genetic predisposition and environment actually work hand in hand together to form who we become. Throw into that the additional power of the will to choose and change our attitudes, and suddenly you see the incredible process by which each of us creates what we call our "self."

Scientists call the process *epigenetics*. This simply means that the expression of our genetic tendencies is turned off or on, accelerated or slowed, by our experiences. Say, for example, a child has a genetic tendency toward anger and violent outbursts. Parents who realize this teach their child to channel this tendency into something positive like playing sports, or they coach the child to take a breath and count to ten before reacting. Or the parent could try to meet violence with violence and pass the family dysfunction on to another generation. If a child has a tendency to be depressed, then parents have the power to teach the child how to find joy in the world and exhibit a more hopeful attitude, or they can isolate the child and drive him or her further into solitude. I believe this is why God gave us parents and why it takes longer for human beings to become adults than any animal on the planet. We need our parents to nurture and direct the way we live and bring us to a point where we can make healthy choices for ourselves. But that is difficult without a great deal of communication and prayerful discipline.

What I want you to see in all of this is that we are not victims of our genetic predispositions, our environment, our minds, or our emotions. Most people don't realize this and fall into the trap of going through the motions and never even nearing the potential God built into them.

A recent Barna Group report stated that over 30 percent of Americans feel "held back or defined by something in their past."[4] David Kinnaman, president of the Barna Group and the director of this study, concluded that "internal doubts about fulfillment, faith, emotion and personal history significantly define millions of the nation's residents."[5] It's as if they feel trapped in a hallway full of locked doors when in fact they have the keys to escape in their pocket but never realize it.

Now I am not saying that our thoughts, our emotions, our past, our relationships, our habits, our addictions, our genetic makeup, and our paradigms are not incredibly powerful influences; what I am saying is that they are not *all*-powerful. God actually designed us so that these things would be influences in our lives for our good—of course, when they become corrupted or painful the opposite happens. However, even after we become adults, epigenetics dictates that changes can still be made. We are, in fact, "captains of [our own] soul[s]," as poet William Ernest Henley penned in 1875, and these "voices"—whether external or internal—are but counselors to the will.[6] Unless it simply acquiesces to these other voices, in the end, Will still gets that final call.

Let's go back again to that little mini-me sitting in the will—the control center—of our souls. In that control center, there are all these gauges, readouts, and screens feeding Mini-me with data, and they are marked "Emotions," "Senses," "Attitude," "Habit," "Memory," "Desires," "Circumstances," "Cravings," and so on. Some of them even have alarms on them that sound so loud they cause us to ignore every other readout until we correct the reading on that gauge.

Mini-me is charged with making decisions. Thus, Mini-me can choose any one of the three options that are basically "yes," "no," or "wait."

Using these options, Mini-me also has the power to react to difficult situations by choosing to quit, conform, or create. Mini-me has the power to look at all of the inputs and readouts for advice—just a few of them, one of them, or even none of them—before making the final call. Mini-me can also take all of it and start processing it in the supercomputer of the prefrontal cortex to weigh out more options and see what remembered wisdom, insight, and knowledge can contribute. Or Mini-me can choose to seek outside counsel. If Will is self-aware and understands the power of stopping in the moment to pay attention to all of this input, it will consider all the options and make better choices. This is the point of contact—the point where decisions are made—that allows us, *through the exercise of our will*, to change our minds, direct our emotions, create better habits, and engineer better futures for both ourselves and those we influence.

Of course, while this is relatively simple to visualize, the practice of it can be somewhat difficult to begin. Sometimes our control centers are rather overloaded, and the alarms on some of our emotions may be so loud that they are hard to choose to ignore for a time, even by the most determined of Wills. We might have grown up in a home where violence was so pervasive that we are literally uncomfortable without it. Strife is so much a part of our upbringing that if we aren't arguing with someone, we find the most insignificant of things to start a fight about so that we will get back to our norm. We may have such low self-esteem that we're afraid to even consider any other dial or readout in the control centers of our minds besides the big sign we've posted that says, "I'm worthless."

If we are going to take control and start the process of living more authentic lives, then a lot of us are going to need a soul makeover before we do anything else. We are going to need someone to come into our control centers and help Mini-me get back on his/her feet, sober up, and learn how to read and interpret all the inputs. We're going to have to poke around and see what needs to be repaired, recognize the patterns that are derailing us, tear down negative attitudes, and start being more aware of our decision-making processes and what is influencing how we act and react as we walk through each day.

The more I have studied this, the more I feel it is a deeply spiritual process. While we can work to train our resolve to begin these changes, the inner strength to accomplish full transformation must come from deeper inside of us. It takes soul searching and heart opening. It takes connecting with the creative power of God. As David expressed the process in the Psalms:

Investigate my life, O God, find out everything about me; cross-examine and test me, get a clear picture of what I'm about; see for Yourself whether I've done anything wrong—then guide me on the road to eternal life.[7]

I believe this is also why Jesus said that the greatest commandment was:

*You shall love the Lord your God with all your **heart**, with all your **soul**, with all your **mind**, and with all your **strength**.*[8]

If we are not pursuing intimacy with God with all of our hearts (spirits), souls, minds (understanding), and strength (bodies), then they are not open to His touch and renovation. This is why spiritual practices such as meditation, prayer, reading the Holy Scriptures, doing good for others, showing kindness and empathy, fasting, and remaining humble and open to hear God's voice are crucial to living authentically. The best way to live the life for which we were designed is to keep ourselves under the constant instruction of the Designer.

Now while the most active changes in our brain take place in the womb, in early childhood, and in adolescence, our minds are much more open to growth later in life than was thought just a decade ago. The "neuroplasticity" of the brain does slow down after the paring down of unused networks and the enhancement of more commonly used neural constructs during adolescence, but that is far from the end of our mental growth as human beings. If we stay active (with regular exercise), consistently practice focusing our attention through activities like prayer and meditation, and frequently seek new learning opportunities in areas we have previously not explored (learn to play an instrument, take up a craft, study a new language, and so forth), our minds stay more limber and open to growth and change. It goes back to the old axiom "use it or lose it," and we all know that "a mind is a terrible thing to waste"—especially your own!

Thus, mental and emotional health are a matter of taking back the control centers of our minds—examining our personal paradigms and confronting the parts of them that hold us back in order to free ourselves to be all we can be; creating habits that build toward success and promote a healthy self-image; molding our attitudes to be positive, open, and loving; and keeping our wills—our mini-mes—alert, mindful, and in the moment so that we are aware of the internal and external inputs influencing us. This allows us to make decisions consciously, rationally, and with compassion.

We were not created to just get by. It was not God's design that some would be leaders and others followers—that some would touch greatness and others would struggle in poverty. He has a plan for each and every one of us for personal achievement, fulfillment, and impact—a plan for self-actualization and abundance. Not only that, but the self-actualization and abundance of others depends on us. The less complete we are in fulfilling our missions on the earth, the more difficult it is for others to fulfill theirs.

If psychological health were measured on a scale of one to ten, I think most of us would be satisfied with being at a seven or an eight, but what you are satisfied with is what you will get. If you expect more and work for more, you will get more. It's an odd juxtaposition of being content in the moment yet ambitious about the future.

I think one of the best representations of this is in the work of Abraham Maslow and his hierarchy of needs. Think of a pyramid with each level building upon the next. The fulfillment of the most basic needs at the bottom of the pyramid is necessary to move to the next level above. (See Diagram D.) Thus, from the bottom up, these needs are:

1. **Physical and biological:** Food, clothing, shelter, sleep, etc.

2. **Environmental safety:** Protection, law, stability, peace, etc.

3. **Belonging:** To be loved, to have solid relationships, be part of a group, etc.

4. **Esteem:** Respect, recognition, achievement, responsibility, etc.

5. **Cognitive:** Knowledge, self-awareness, meaning, etc.

6. **Aesthetic:** Balance, experiencing beauty, seeing in new ways, etc.

7. **Self-actualization:** Growth, fulfillment, creativity, spirituality, etc.

8. **Transcendence:** Contributing to the self-actualization of others.

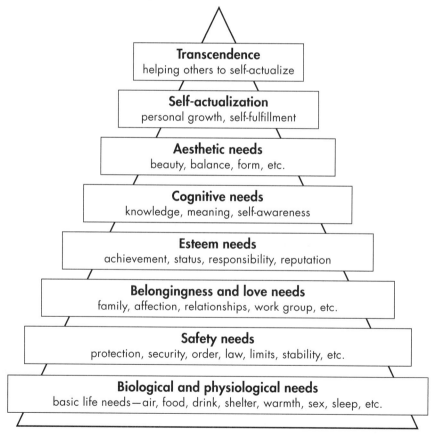

Diagram D

Each of these depends upon us having a will that can make conscious, wise, and unbiased decisions. It is having a will that is truly free—not overwhelmed by our pasts, not trapped in patterns and habits that are self-destructive, nor enslaved to emotions or addictions—that exists in a paradigm that is ethical, hopeful, confident, and open to possibilities.

It also means living a life that is congruent and not compartmentalized. It means our activities Sunday through Saturday share purpose, significance, and focus—they are things we can do in each moment with all of our soul without compromising integrity or authenticity. They frame lives that can hear from and live by the Spirit as regularly as they hear the physical voices of others and interact in the tactile world.

"OK," you may be saying, "but I'm not exactly close to that kind of life. That all sounds so wonderful, but how do I get there from here? What am I supposed to do with all of this knowledge you are passing along here?"

Well, as I have said before, it is all about what you pay attention to. It's time for you to stop just spending your life and learn to start investing it.

Quantum physics suggests that by redirecting our focus— where we place our attention—we bring a new course of events into focus while at the same time releasing an existing course of events that may no longer serve us.

—GREGG BRADEN, *THE ISAIAH EFFECT*

It matters not how strait the gate, how charged with punishments the scroll, I am the master of my fate: I am the captain of my soul.

—WILLIAM EARNEST HENLEY, "INVICTUS"

History maker arise...and think deliberately about the power of your decisions.

You have the power of choice when it comes to your response to difficult situations. When you stop and think deliberately about the available options, you will make better choices. Created with free will, you can change your mind, control and direct your emotions, form better habits, and build improved futures for yourself and for those you influence.

Influence affects people negatively or positively. It is incumbent upon you to use your power of influence by recognizing it is a deeply spiritual process, not in any way superficial.

When taking the time to think about the importance of your decisions and the inner strength it takes to accomplish full transformation, it means searching your soul and opening your heart—but most of all, connecting with the creative power of God who will direct your path: *"You make known to me the path of life; You will fill me with joy in Your presence, with eternal pleasures at Your right hand."*[9]

History maker arise...and pray for focus.

What you pay attention to matters. When you stop *spending* your life and start *investing* it, the difference will be undeniably more significant and impactful—for you and others. Pray that your heavenly Father will help you move swiftly up the "needs" ladder, absorbing each for its particular value then climbing up to where you are balanced, creative, growing, and seeking to genuinely contribute to the self-actualization of others.

Pray that the Holy Spirit will help you make thoughtful, astute, and impartial decisions, full of power, confidence, and sincerely motivated for the good of all. Prayerfully determine to focus your attention on God's Word and constantly pursue new learning opportunities, keeping your mind open to the development and advancement of people inside and outside your current sphere of influence.

CHAPTER SEVEN

principles of investment

This is the first, the wildest and the wisest thing I know: that the soul exists and is built entirely out of attentiveness.

—MARY OLIVER

Healing the universe is an inside job.

—*MINDWALK*

Whatever you set your attention on affects your life—in fact, good or bad, it increases in value. Think about that for a moment. What do most people spend their time doing? Lots of people spend hours every day watching television, and it is one of the largest industries in America. People spend time shopping, and retailers make money. Though it is a closet activity and unhealthy for the soul, millions of Americans surf the Internet looking at pornography, and the industry has skyrocketed. Such sites prey on the basest instincts of humanity, siphoning off self-esteem and money, but because people spend their time doing it, good or bad, others make huge amounts of money from it.

The truth of the matter is, whether you are Elon Musk, Melinda Gates, unemployed, or homeless, we all only have three things we can invest—our time, our talent, or our treasure. Oddly enough, the most valuable of these three is the very thing everyone has exactly the same amount of—time. Whether we are captains of industry, workers on an assembly line, or children at play, we all have no more or less than 24 hours a day, 7 days a week, and 52 weeks a year. However, it is what we focus on during those hours, days, and weeks that either makes our time more valuable or less valuable. There is a reason a fast food worker makes minimum wage and a high-powered attorney makes hundreds of dollars an hour. One has invested more time in education and learning than the other, making the time they invest now pay a higher dividend in return.

Although we all have the same amount of time, we have a choice about whether we will spend it, waste it, or invest it in learning, honing skills, praying, meditating, or helping others. We can genuinely interact with others, or we can abuse our relationships or take them for granted. We have the choice of pursuing growth for the bulk of each day with some downtime to recharge our batteries, or we can whine and complain about our work or our studies because they interfere with our play. It doesn't take a rocket scientist to figure out which one's talents and treasure will grow the fastest.

It reminds me of a story that world-renowned salesman and motivational speaker Zig Ziglar used to tell about how your intentions impact your destiny. It's such a great story; I wouldn't be surprised if you've already heard it. However, just in case you haven't, I want to share it again here:

On a stretch of railroad track some men were working hard under the sun. A beautiful private train came by, and a man shouted from inside the train in excitement, "Hey Old Jim! Is that you?"

Old Jim, who was hard at work, looked up and replied, "Hi Joe! That's me alright!"

"Jim, why don't you come in here for a cup of coffee?"

Jim hurried in with joy as the sun was hot and he wanted to get into the air-conditioned cabin of this beautiful train. After about an hour or so, Jim came out with Joe and they hugged as old friends would and parted ways. When the train left, the people around asked Jim, "Hey Old Jim, isn't that Joe Murphy, the president of our railway?"

"Sure he is, we have been friends for twenty years now. In fact, we've known each other since the first day we started together working on the railroad."

"What?! How is it then that he is now the president of the railway, while you are still working here?"

"The answer is very simple. On the first day that we came to work, I came to work for $3.50 per hour, but Joe Murphy came to build a railway."[1]

In his book *Outliers*, Malcolm Gladwell discusses the "Matthew effect," which is based on Matthew 25:29:

For to everyone who has, more will be given, and he will have abundance; but from him who does not have, even what he has will be taken away.[2]

In other words, success breeds success. Relationships matter immensely, for those who are associated with the successful find opportunities that others don't. Favor leads to favor. The more we apply our time as an investment building our assets, rather than treating it as currency to be exchanged for being entertained, the more we are ready when opportunity knocks. As the old adage goes, success happens when preparation meets opportunity.

However, there is another adage in the Bible that is even more important: *"Every good gift and every perfect gift is from above, and comes down from the Father of lights, with whom there is no variation or shadow of turning."*[3] Another way to say this is that God is not going to bless us with things that will ultimately become curses. He simply cannot do it. It is against His very nature. Thus as we invest our time to gain wisdom and knowledge, we must also exemplify ethics and character; otherwise the financial and material blessings we obtain will only be from our own efforts and not from God. When God blesses, *"The blessing of the Lord makes rich, and He adds no sorrow with it."*[4]

It is possible to get rich without ethics and character, but impossible to live a rich life![5] I study and speak a great deal on how to maximize potential in order to fulfill purpose—and in doing so to live the abundant life Jesus came to provide.[6] I believe the process of converting potential into performance happens when character is translated into behaviors that are practiced every day. People who gain wealth without character only multiply their troubles because of the increased pressure that comes with increased affluence. Too often they end up even more miserable than they were when they had little. On the other hand, God gives wealth to be a blessing to us—and so that we can be a blessing to others.

The mistake we make is looking at some future "someday" as the answer to our current life situation without realizing that the answers we need are already in hand. For example, we already have as much time in a day to invest as we will ever have in a day—as much time to learn, as much time to get a project done, as much time to spend with our loved ones, as much time to plan for our futures, and so forth—as we will ever have in a day or a week. If we use it wisely, we grow, and tomorrow's time will have incrementally more talent and value added to it; if we waste it, then we will simply have to start tomorrow what we could have started today. As Jesus said:

If you are faithful in little things, you will be faithful in large ones. But if you are dishonest in little things, you won't be honest with greater responsibilities. And if you are untrustworthy about worldly wealth, who will trust you with the true riches of heaven? And if you are not faithful with other people's things, why should you be trusted with things of your own?[7]

How you view your world and what you already have is so important. Do you count your failures, or do you count your blessings? Do you look at a glass as half full or half empty? (And by the way, I have a secret for you—the glass is actually completely full, half with water and half with air, both of which are crucial to our lives!) Do you have everything you need to take your next step in God's plan for you—or every time you think of that step, do you start counting what you don't have and then end up so discouraged that you just shelve your hopes?

I believe that God likes to multiply more than add. God is a 30-, 60-, 100-fold type of Creator, not a plus one, plus two, plus three type of Blesser. But you know what a hundred times nothing is? Still nothing. God can multiply only what you have, not what you need. When Jesus was faced with a crowd of 5,000 hungry people, did He create food out of thin air to feed them? No, He took a little boy's lunch of five barley loaves and two fishes that were given to Him and multiplied it to feed the multitude.[8] Do you have the attitude of the little boy? He looked at what he had and decided to share it rather than saying it was not enough. Do you look at what you have and think it's not enough to get you where you want to be and, therefore, refuse to even start? Or do you turn to God and say, "Here is what I have—how do I use this to get where You want me to go?" It doesn't matter how little you start with but what you do with it.

Do you have such a sufficiency? I believe the answer to that question is "yes."

Did you know that the Greek word translated *sufficiency*—αὐτάρκεια—appears in the same form only one other place in the New Testament? That is in First Timothy 6:6, where it is translated *contentment*: "*Now godliness with **contentment** is great gain.*"[9] Another translation of the word would be "enough." It seems to be a concept the apostle Paul understood, for in another place, he says:

> *Not that I speak in regard to need, for I have learned in whatever state I am, to be content: I know how to be abased, and I know how to abound. Everywhere and in all things I have learned both to be full and to be hungry, both to abound and to suffer need. I can do all things through Christ who strengthens me.*[10]

If you can look around you and see what you have on hand and say, "With God and what I have here, I have enough to do whatever He has called me to do," then I am telling you, you are starting in exactly the right place. You may have a long way to go, but now, in this moment, you are content; you have enough. God has met your every need. It is an attitude that will keep you right—whether you have a little or a lot. God isn't against your having stuff, but neither is He in favor of your being so caught up with your stuff that it has you!

When God brings a blessing of increased wealth to a person, it is because He knows that it won't corrupt that person. Then, as that person becomes more excited about God's mission for his or her life, God looks for more ways to get wealth into that person's hands so that the Kingdom of God can continue to grow. That Kingdom is where God's will is done and His goodness is seen. It is a place where there is no sickness, no lack—a place of equal opportunity and brotherly love. It is a place where things simply work right. It is the place where the investment of your time, talents, and treasure pays off for you as well as those around you. But to get there, you can't despise starting right where you are right now, even if it seems impossible to get to your dream destination from here.

R. G. LeTourneau was just the kind of guy who didn't mind small beginnings. Born in November 1888, Robert Gilmour LeTourneau was restless, curious, determined, and ambitious, living in a time when automobiles were just coming into common use. Being about six feet tall and 160 pounds as a seventh grader, R. G. decided he had had enough of school. Rather than balking at this, his parents found him the toughest job they could, one they thought would have him running back to school after just a few days. It didn't work, however. He took to working at the steel mill like a duck to water.

He wouldn't avoid getting an education though. It just wouldn't be in a schoolhouse. R. G. diligently applied himself to whatever he could do with tools in his hands. He worked as an iron molder, a machinist, a welder, and a mechanic. The work in the machine shop at the steel mill so fascinated him that rather than going home after a hard day of work, he stuck around until late in the evenings, learning how to use the machines and designing and building his own small steam engine. When others complained about how fast industry was changing at the turn of the 20th century and saw it as a difficulty, R. G. was instead fascinated. He allowed change to be his routine. It presented more things to mess around with and see if he could make better. He became a master at inventing things out of whatever happened to be lying around.

Eventually he got into earthmoving and road building. Of course, the machines that he bought to do the work were never good enough, so he modified them. He would often work during the day moving earth and then be so absorbed by what he wanted to improve that he would work on inventing a solution until late at night so he could try it out the next day. Other times he would simply start from scratch to build his own machines, working from the designs he had floating around in his head. He never stopped tinkering and improving.

R. G. was the first person to think to put a blade on the front of a tractor to make a bulldozer because, up until that time, everything was still based on earthmovers that had been pulled by horses or mules. All they had done was replace the animals with tractors. Throughout his lifetime, he built one of the biggest and most innovative earthmoving equipment companies the world has ever known.

He was so wealthy that during the last several years of his life he gave away 90 percent of his income and lived off the remaining 10 percent! When asked how he could do that year after year and still keep getting richer, he smiled and confessed, "I keep shoveling it out, and God keeps shoveling it right back in—and He has a bigger shovel!"[11] Quite a statement for a man who built the biggest "shovels" the world has ever seen!

Throughout his lifetime, R. G. was a man of unified purpose.[12] For him, his work with earthmoving and then building and selling earthmoving machines literally paved the way to better transportation, less expensive and fresher foods, and more jobs as these things helped businesses grow. Yet this went hand in hand with sending money overseas to missionaries to bring medicine, public health, and improved agriculture as well as spiritual enrichment to impoverished nations. R. G. worshiped in his shops, working late exercising his creativity, just as he worshiped in church on Sunday mornings.

Not only that, but I believe, just as it did for George Washington Carver and others like him, that R. G.'s faith and sense of purpose fueled his inventiveness and creativity. Though the term hadn't been coined yet, they were the "social entrepreneurs" of their generation. Their lives of the spirit and compassionate hearts gave wisdom to their minds and souls, and they reveled in their work as if it was a calling to ministry—which it was—not just a job to make ends meet.

Are you plugging into your spirit for the ideas that will change your world? Are you disciplining your mind, will, and emotions to be open to your spiritual nature to find answers to the problems that confront you? Spirituality is not just so that you can feel better about life, finding personal fulfillment in "self-actualization"—because the highest level of Maslow's hierarchy is not about your fulfillment but about you helping others to find theirs.

If the God we follow is the Creator of all, don't you think He would have some fixes for whatever difficulties we face? I am not talking about miracles either, even though I love miracles. I am talking about day-to-day living in connection with your human spirit that is in tune with the Spirit of God so that whatever ideas, inventions, favor, poise, determination, or compassion you need manifests in your life as you live out His dreams for you. This is the life of personal and social transformation, and it is the best kind of life you can live.

Author of *Making Hope Happen*, Dr. Shane Lopez, writes about the effects of setting even the tiniest ripple of hope into motion:

> You don't have to take big, bold action or raise a ton of money
> to spark change. You can start small. You merely need to
> create momentum where there was none.[13]

And that momentum is what drives the currents of change we're striving to create. "Making ripples starts with you," Lopez writes.[14]

You know that irksome feeling you get when you see a problem that no one is doing anything about? Or the pang you feel when someone is left behind by life? That's where you start.[15]

You are given clues on a daily basis about the waves you can start making—beginning with the smallest ripples of hope you set in motion. A kind word, a generous deed, or a listening ear can spread hope. Any action you take to positively influence the people or atmosphere around you—any positive response that counters the pervasive indifference plaguing our society—positions you to become the kind of leader the world so desperately needs.

Just as we have to be ready to dream new communities, so we have to be willing to dream new selves. We have to be willing to know that we can become much more than we have ever been. And that in itself, in some situations, would be considered a spiritual kind of calling. It is also a political calling to know that our job is not an impossible job; that we have the capacity to do what is necessary to be done.

—Vincent Harding

History maker arise...and invest in yourself and others.

Plugging into your spirit prompts God to trigger ideas in your mind that you can use to change your world. Disciplining your mind, will, and emotions opens your spiritual nature to solve problems confronting you—and the world around you. Feeling better about life and finding personal fulfillment in "self-actualization" is ultimately about helping others find their purpose.

Choosing to connect with others in your day-to-day living attracts the Spirit of God so that whatever ideas, inventions, favor, poise, determination, and compassion you need will manifest in your life. Choose today to reach out in love to inspire someone else to dream—as you live out God's dreams for you. Interrelating with others promotes interconnection with God, who loves to invest in a "sure thing"—*you!*

Christ told the parable of investing, saying to the one who doubled his talents, *"Well done, good and faithful servant; you were faithful over a few things, I will make you ruler over many things. Enter into the joy of your lord."*[16] Wise investing brings rewards.

History maker arise...and pray for greater leadership capacity.

Dear Lord, shower me with clues that will lead me to invest myself in currents of active change in the world. Help me see the next steps to take to positively influence the people and the circumstances around me. I realize that any positive movement that counters the pervasive indifference plaguing our society will further Your Kingdom on earth, refreshing it with waves of life-giving nourishment.

Father God, the world needs leaders who are devoted to guiding others with humbleness and a trustworthiness beyond reproach. I pray, Father, that You will raise me to the position You deem me ready to fulfill. Amen.

CHAPTER EIGHT

being known

How we connect with others has unimagined significance.

—DANIEL GOLEMAN, *SOCIAL INTELLIGENCE*

*Too often we underestimate the power of a touch,
a smile, a kind word, a listening ear, an honest
accomplishment, or the smallest act of caring, all of which
have the potential to turn a life around.*

—LEO BUSCAGLIA, *LOVE*

On September 9, 2003, the Commission on Children at Risk in Washington, DC, released a series of papers discussing the growth of some disconcerting trends among adolescents in the United States. Despite growing up in the most affluent country in the world and living through one of the most prosperous decades in history (the 1990s), typical American high schoolers were reporting more anxiety and neuroses than did children who were psychiatric patients in the 1950s.[1] The World Health Organization estimated that about 1 in every

12 suffered from clinical depression.[2] The previous year, roughly 1 out of every 5 students had reported seriously considering committing suicide.[3] It had been reported that in Midwestern universities—those in the very heartland of the United States—over the previous 13 years, the number of students who sought counseling for depression had doubled, the number of suicidal students had tripled, and the number of those seen after sexual assaults had quadrupled.[4] Members of the National Research Council estimated from the evidence they had in hand that one out of every four adolescents in the United States was at risk of not achieving a productive adulthood.[5]

Meanwhile, the children of immigrant families did not suffer from these ills, despite the fact that many of them had lower socio-economic levels than the average American. However, the longer these families were in the United States, the more their children suffered from the same psychosomatic illnesses as their peers.

The report went on to state:

It is important to note that most of this good news is linked to broad recent improvements in our *material* wellbeing, which in turn are closely connected to the astonishing economic growth that characterized most of the 1990s, as well as to impressive recent drops in US crime rates. We are heartened by these changes. But *despite them*, US young people not only appear to be experiencing sharp increases in mental illness and stress and emotional problems but also continue to suffer from high—we as a commission believe unacceptably high— rates of related behavioral problems such as substance abuse, school dropout, interpersonal violence, premature sexual intercourse, and teenage pregnancy.[6]

To address these issues, the research team looked at everything from social trends to the latest research on the development of the brain to the effects of the nurturing habits of prairie voles and rhesus monkeys regarding how their offspring interacted socially. What they found was that while there were cultural influences and environmental

issues that contributed to these problems, these were minor compared
to one constant: *those who had the most stable intergenerational
connections also exhibited the best mental health*. The report found that
adolescents needed strong connections to parents or strong mentors
who had a solid framework (worldview) of meaning in their lives. In
other words, the key to addressing the concerns of the risky behavior
being exhibited lay in the adolescents being connected with others and
having a growing sense of purpose in their lives. People have a basic
need to feel loved, to be healthy, and to believe their existence has
meaning, or as the researchers of this report described it:

> First, a great deal of evidence shows that we are hardwired
> for close attachments to other people, beginning with our
> mothers, fathers, and extended family, and then moving out
> to the broader community.
>   Second, a less definitive but still significant body of
> evidence suggests that we are hardwired for meaning, born
> with a built-in capacity and drive to search for purpose and
> reflect on life's ultimate ends.[7]

As the report describes it, human beings are not designed to
live solitary, disconnected lives—and doing so leads to emotional
and psychological "difficulties" at best. Though cultural changes and
modernization contributed to the problems that inspired this report,
the commission wasn't looking to try to institute a number of laws and
policies that would remedy these adverse social trends. They decided to
try to change the conversation that was going on around childrearing
and see if parents, educators, and youth workers wouldn't then act
according to what they valued. Rather than being swept along in
the river of social norms that seemed to lead to increased feelings of
disconnection and isolation, they would focus on strengthening families
and community organizations that gave young people healthy places to
learn, grow, and connect with others.

Searching for the answer to a parallel set of questions, the Search
Institute, an organization that has been researching what helps children
and adolescents become caring, responsible, successful adults for more

than 50 years, has developed what they call the Forty Developmental Assets®. The more of these assets that exist in a child's life, the more likely they are to do the things that lead to being contributing citizens and not doing the things that make them burdens to society.

The following is the list of assets with brief descriptions:[8]

EXTERNAL ASSETS

Support

1. **Family support**—Family life provides high levels of love and support.

2. **Positive family communication**—Young person and her or his parent(s) communicate positively, and young person is willing to seek advice and counsel from parents.

3. **Other adult relationships**—Young person receives support from three or more nonparent adults.

4. **Caring neighborhood**—Young person experiences caring neighbors.

5. **Caring school climate**—School provides a caring, encouraging environment.

Empowerment

6. **Parent involvement in schooling**—Parents are actively involved in helping young person succeed in school.

7. **Community values youth**—Young person perceives that adults in the community value youth.

8. **Youth as resources**—Young people are given useful roles in the community.

9. **Service to others**—Young person serves in the community one hour or more per week.

10. **Safety**—Young person feels safe at home, school, and in the neighborhood.

Boundaries and Expectations

11. **Family boundaries**—Family has clear rules and consequences and monitors the young person's whereabouts.

12. **School boundaries**—School provides clear rules and consequences.

13. **Neighborhood boundaries**—Neighbors take responsibility for monitoring young people's behavior.

14. **Adult role models**—Parent(s) and other adults model positive, responsible behavior.

15. **Positive peer influence**—Young person's best friends model responsible behavior.

Constructive Use of Time

16. **High expectations**—Both parent(s) and teachers encourage the young person to do well.

17. **Creative activities**—Young person spends three or more hours per week in lessons or practice in music, theater, or other arts.

18. **Youth programs**—Young person spends three or more hours per week in sports, clubs, or organizations at school and/or in the community.

19. **Religious community**—Young person spends one or more hours per week in activities in a religious institution.

20. **Time at home**—Young person is out with friends "with nothing special to do" two or fewer nights per week.

INTERNAL ASSETS

Commitment to Learning

21. **Achievement motivation**—Young person is motivated to do well in school.

22. **School engagement**—Young person is actively engaged in learning.

23. **Homework**—Young person reports doing at least one hour of homework every school day.

24. **Bonding to school**—Young person cares about her or his school.

25. **Reading for pleasure**—Young person reads for pleasure three or more hours per week.

Positive Values

26. **Caring**—Young person places high value on helping other people.

27. **Equality and social justice**—Young person places high value on promoting equality and reducing hunger and poverty.

28. **Integrity**—Young person acts on convictions and stands up for her or his beliefs.

29. **Honesty**—Young person "tells the truth even when it is not easy."

30. **Responsibility**—Young person accepts and takes personal responsibility.

Social Competencies

31. **Restraint**—Young person believes it is important not to be sexually active or to use alcohol or other drugs.

32. **Planning and decision-making**—Young person knows how to plan ahead and make choices.

33. **Interpersonal competence**—Young person has empathy, sensitivity, and friendship skills.

34. **Cultural competence**—Young person has knowledge of and comfort with people of different cultural/racial/ethnic backgrounds.

35. **Resistance skills**—Young person can resist negative peer pressure and dangerous situations.

Positive Identity

36. **Peaceful conflict resolution**—Young person seeks to resolve conflict nonviolently.

37. **Personal power**—Young person feels he or she has control over "things that happen to me."

38. **Self-esteem**—Young person reports having a high self-esteem.

39. **Sense of purpose**—Young person reports that "my life has a purpose."

40. **Positive view of personal future**—Young person is optimistic about her or his personal future.

The more of these assets kids have in their lives, the better they do in school; the more likely they are to exhibit leadership, be in good health, and value diversity; and the less likely they are to be involved in drug and alcohol abuse, exhibit violent behavior, or engage in premature sexual activity. The reason for this is the web of protection and purpose these assets build around and within young people. They are the basis for communities that help children grow into productive, contributing adults, and they are values that every productive, contributing adult should exhibit as they both follow their own purposes and act as leaders in their communities.

These values are universal for communities the world round. While our overall cultures may have some great ills, the foundational building blocks that lead to a better tomorrow are not all that complicated. It just takes responsible individuals getting involved in the lives of their children, their children's friends, and the children in their communities. It has to do with individuals connecting with individuals and building mutual confidence, purpose, and work ethic to realize the potential God has put into them.

While books and programs are wonderful, empowerment comes more often from other people who inspire, pass along wisdom, and discipline—teachers, activity leaders, youth directors, children supervisors, aunts and uncles, grandparents, and so forth. The true riches of any community are not its possessions but its ability to adapt and grow from the ideas of its own citizens. Individuals and communities alike thrive when individuals are free to choose for themselves, create for themselves, and contribute to others within the framework of healthy social and personal relationships.

It all starts with changing mind-sets. We must place valuing relationships near the top of our lists, and that starts with first changing our own ways of thinking and acting. We must learn to hold above all things our relationship with God, then with our families, then with coworkers on the job and at church, and then on out from there to our communities, nations, and world.

As human beings, we have an essential need inside of us to deeply connect with God and with others. We are social creatures who thrive best when we are deeply known and, in being known, deeply loved. It is what creates the foundation for a healthy self-image from which we can reach out to others and have the courage to accomplish great things. It is a need for intimacy—not necessarily of body, but of the soul.

While this is a foundational, basic need, it is also the one that holds most of us back from believing in ourselves enough to accomplish our dreams in a healthy way. If we do not have these kinds of relationships with our parents as we grow through our formative years, we are likely to be people who constantly question our self-worth without ever really being conscious of why. If we do not connect with the teacher or youth worker who cares and inspires, we are even more unlikely to reach for our dreams. If we have never felt true love and acceptance from others, how are we ever to love and accept ourselves? Without these relationships, we feel rejection so centrally at our core that it often becomes lodged in our unconscious. We create ties on the *soulular* level that leech energy, confidence, and enthusiasm out of our lives instead of being foundations upon which to add value and increase them. It is like the gauges for "believing in ourselves" and "having self-confidence" are taped over in Mini-me's little control room. They are so fundamentally absent from our lives that we don't even know to look for them. We become like ships without an anchor, adrift in unfriendly waters.

We so long for this sense of assurance and acceptance that we try to connect with almost anyone to get it, and this often leads to our ending up in one empty and hurtful relationship after another. We develop what I call an "orphan spirit," or an attitude that causes us to believe that no matter what, we are unwanted, unacceptable, and unlovable. Our bad relationship patterns reinforce this, causing a downward spiral toward even less healthy relationships and the desire to anesthetize our lives with addictions and other self-destructive behaviors. An orphaned heart is a hurting heart. It makes us more susceptible to disease, distraction, disorder, and dysfunction. It stresses our system in such small, incremental ways that we don't even notice until something major breaks down in our lives.

The good news, however, is that orphaned hearts can be healed. Coming into a closer relationship with the God who is Love is priority one, whether we had loving parents or not.[9] We must open our hearts and souls to God and *let Him love on us*. We must allow ourselves to bathe in the light of His love. The metaphor of God as *"our Father"* is one used to show His nurturing, loving, and disciplining nature for those of us who are *"His children."* To get a full understanding of God as *the* loving Father is spiritual revolution. It has the power to turn our whole world upside right.

Once we consciously acknowledge the power that the orphan spirit has in our lives, we can begin to overcome it. We can begin to choose different thoughts—those that recognize we are fully known, fully accepted, fully forgiven, and fully loved by God—and so much so that God didn't hold back His Son from doing what it took to be connected with us. We must meditate on the Scriptures that speak of His love for us and let them renew our self-image and transform the way we think. Making the most of resources such as my other soul series books, *The 40 Day Soul Fast, Reclaim Your Soul,* and *The Prosperous Soul,* along with their companion devotionals and curriculums, will help you break through the clutter and excess baggage of your life so you can see yourself as God sees you. You need to be confident and whole in the love the Father has for you. Recognize your own potential and start taking those first steps down the road to being the person of God's dreams!

One of those steps will be taking inventory of the relationships in your life. Some will need to be cut off, others can be repaired and redeemed, and others will grow into trusted and cherished mutual supports. To have good friends, you must be capable of *being* a good friend—and that means with your coworkers, neighbors, and spouse! You do not necessarily stay close to someone with whom you have been physically intimate, but those who are "kindred spirits" or "soul mates" will be with you for a lifetime if you continue to nurture those relationships.

Not every relationship will be that deep, of course, but if you have solid relationships in place, then you will have more freedom in trusting more casual acquaintances and interactions as well. Showing kindness and courtesy is the oil that keeps the wheels of culture and business running smoothly. In your day-to-day interactions—even with complete strangers—what are you communicating about how you value peace and compassion in your life? Are you stressing and messing or coalescing and blessing? Are you a weight on others or a relief for them? Are your interactions with others extending the influence of the goodness of God or proof to them that hypocrisy is a way of life for people "of faith"?

You cannot be all you can be without strong relationships. Strong families are built upon the quality of the relationships within them, and strong family relationships contribute to stronger communities and churches and thus to stronger cities and nations. Businesses either grow or are limited by their ability to coordinate, unite, create, connect, and organize around specific ideas and products. Innovation dies in places where more time is spent on competition and distrust than on cooperation and trust. If our goal is to make a positive impact on our world, we must learn to be leaders—first of ourselves and then of others. True leadership is about serving, not about giving orders—it's not about titles and lines of authority, nor is it about the biggest office or the highest salary; it's about influence. You don't have to look far to discover that there are a lot of people promoted into positions to supervise groups and divisions who have little or no leadership ability at all (and most suffer for it), while there are people you would follow even if all they did was deliver the mail. They have the abilities needed to get good ideas across and inspire effectiveness in others, even if they don't have company-recognized authority.

If we want to be such leaders, it is not about the next promotion at work or getting the pastor to call and ask us to be on the board of elders; we have to step in and start being the type of leader Jesus was. We have to first recognize who we are in relationship to the Father and all He has endowed us with in order to fully live into that—and then we must start becoming the people whom He has called us to be. It means learning to lead ourselves rather than trying to find people to tell us what to do. It means becoming healthy souls so that we can "win souls" to the causes God has given us. As it says in Proverbs, *"The fruit of righteousness is a tree of life, and he who wins souls is wise."*[10] Living fully and authentically as the world changers God created us to be is the foundation of a fulfilled life. But we must first change the world within through strong self-leadership. When others see our lives, they see there is something to follow. It is thus our responsibility, as we grow in God, not only to be the type of leaders God can promote, but also to have a purpose in our lives worth leading other people toward. As Stephen Covey said:

I am personally convinced that one person can be a change
catalyst, a "transformer" in any situation, any organization
once they are individuals of character. Such an individual
is yeast that can leaven an entire loaf. It requires vision,
initiative, patience, respect, persistence, courage, and faith to
be a transforming leader.[11]

That leader has to know who they are and live true to that.

Essentially, this book is about becoming that "change catalyst."
Up to this point, we have delved into the life of the soul and explored
how our interior state of being—whether well and whole or wounded
and despairing—affects the state of the world. It is my hope that you
have learned some life-altering—or at least mind-altering—principles
in reading so far, but also that you will read other authors in more
depth about these subjects so that you can gain mastery over your own
mind, will, and emotions. Why? Because when you do, you will begin
stirring those ripples of hope within your soul that drive the currents
of cultural change throughout the world.

We can never be reminded enough that Jesus' instructions were
not only about our own personal success and stability, but were also
about expanding His Kingdom by creating places where His goodness
and love are the rule instead of the exception. We have to find the
innovations we need to lift people out of poverty and famine and
discover the keys to changing the mind-sets of those bent by hatred
and generations of prejudice and fear. We must apply the principles of
soul healing to our communities and nations. While none of this may
be easy, we also know that *"nothing will be impossible with God."*[12]

Although there is still a great deal more to be discussed about
these topics that we do not have space for here, we need to transition
now to taking these principles to the next level—not only to the wider
global community, but also farther generationally. We need to go from
self-leadership and learning how to lead others to shaping history;

from personal innovation and paradigm shifting to creating a cultural revolution on a global and multigenerational scale. The challenge we have in front of us for the 21st century is an immense one, but also the most exciting history has ever seen.

We are living in history-defining times. At no other time has the world been so interconnected or has information traveled across the planet at the speed of thought. Within nanoseconds, we can know of an individual's need in a remote area on the other side of the globe, and if we can't meet that need within a matter of hours, we can intercede through prayer in a matter of seconds. Solving problems and meeting needs is where purpose is found and fulfilled. Fulfilling God's purpose is why you and I are here—both collectively as the Body of Christ and individually as Christ's disciples. We get a sense of that purpose where we see Jesus announce:

The Spirit of the Lord is upon Me, because He has anointed
Me to preach the gospel to the poor; He has sent Me to heal the
brokenhearted, to proclaim liberty to the captives and recovery
of sight to the blind, to set at liberty those who are oppressed;
to proclaim the acceptable year of the Lord.[13]

We must embrace that purpose as our own—and make it central to all we do in this world.

It is time to get out of our comfort zones and make a difference. It is time to become the shapers of history we were born on this planet at this time in history to be. The world—in fact, the entire universe—is counting on us to do so.

Our goal is to create a beloved community, and this will
require a qualitative change in our souls as well
as a quantitative change in our lives.

—Dr. Martin Luther King Jr.

History maker arise...to accept your role in mentoring the lives of others.

As a perfectly planned person designed to bring order and civility to a chaotic world, you can help provide the web of protection and purpose in and around younger generations when you accept your God-chosen role in community life. Knowing how vital it is for people, especially young people, to feel loved and "known" and the values and factors that help children grow into productive, contributing adults, you can lean in, nudging them in the right direction.

While it may seem that your immediate society has too many faults to mention, the fundamentals that lead to better tomorrows are easier than you may think. It just takes responsible individuals—like you—getting involved in the lives of youngsters. With whom can you connect to start building mutual confidence, purpose, and a work ethic to realize the potential God has placed within them? "If you can't feed a hundred people, then just feed one," said Mother Teresa. Who is the one you can feed with love and recognition today?

History maker arise...as a pray-er for fellow sojourners.

James says, *"Therefore confess your sins to each other and pray for each other so that you may be healed. The prayer of a righteous person is powerful and effective."*[14] No one is above having sins to confess—doing so brings relief to the soul. And no one is above needing healing for myriad pain and suffering.

Even Jesus Christ offered up prayers and petitions to His Father with fervent cries and tears to the One He knew could save Him.[15]

As you pray today, lift up to God those you know, and don't know, who need His healing touch—physical, mental, spiritual, relational—and believe your prayer is heard and answered. Intercessory prayer is one of the most valuable weapons in your arsenal when combatting satan, who delights in blocking youth from becoming upstanding young men and women.[16]

PART THREE

SHAPING HISTORY

Respect, I think, always implies imagination—the ability to see one another, across our inevitable differences [socio-geopolitical borders and multigenerational spans of time], as living souls.

—WENDELL BERRY

A sense of community is the holy grail of modern living...when we cannot find it in the present day, we reach back through the years and say, "That was when we knew each other, that was when we held all things in common." ...it is the thought so tender and consoling that it scarcely matters if it's not true.

—*CALL THE MIDWIFE*

CHAPTER NINE

from "i" to "us" without a "them"

*You have heard that it was said, "Love your neighbor
and hate your enemy." But I tell you, love your enemies
and pray for those who persecute you, that you
may be children of your Father in heaven.*

—MATTHEW 5:43–45 NIV

*My continuing passion is to part a curtain, that
invisible shadow that falls between people,
the veil of indifference to each other's presence,
each other's wonder, each other's human plight.*

—EUDORA WELTY, ONE TIME, ONE PLACE

In a recent conversation I had with Phil Clothier of the Barrett Values Centre, he gave me an example of how we need to expand our views of influence in the world:

In the village here [in England], we've got a place between
the trees and the river where the teenagers park their cars
and eat their fast food. When they've eaten their fast food,
they've got a problem. They've got trash in their car. At that
moment, their world is only as big as the inside of their car, so
this problem is not really a problem at all. All they need to do
is wind down the window, and throw the trash out. Then they
can wind the window back up, and "My world is clean again.
This is all working for me." Because we all like a clean world,
and this got their world clean again.

Now, if they get to the level of consciousness where they
associate themselves with the size of the village, then my
hope would be they would drive to the next village and throw
the trash out there [he said chuckling facetiously].

The point here is that the bigger the world with which you associate
yourself, the more your personal values will show up in that community.

During World War II, loving family men in Germany went off each
day to the concentration camps where they tortured and murdered
Jews, extracted their teeth for the gold in them, used their skin to
make lampshades, rifled through their clothes and possessions for
whatever they could find of value, and then dumped their bodies into
mass graves as if merely emptying one more wheelbarrow full of dirt.
Every day they saw emaciated men, women, and children struggling
for existence, and they were more inclined to show them the butt of
their rifles than a helping hand. At home, children laughed and played
with fathers who they only knew as officers working to protect their
homeland, while on the job, these men were something quite different
indeed. It was a schizophrenic existence at best.

In Israel there is a huge fence being built along the edges of the
West Bank between the Palestinian and Israeli "territories." This fence
routinely cuts miles into the West Bank because the Israelis feel that
is the distance they need to keep their villages and settlements safe.
In some places, it has divided Palestinian farmers and shepherds from
the land their families have used for generations. Some such cases

have gone to Israeli courts, and the fence has been moved to restore the Palestinian rights.

Near Jerusalem, every Friday, this fence is the scene of conflict. Palestinians wearing gas masks on one side throw rocks at Israeli soldiers; and on the other side, the soldiers shoot at the protestors with water cannons and tear gas. The water has something in it to give it a foul smell to further deter the attackers. When they can, the Palestinians will bring in construction vehicles to try to tear at the fence. For the Israelis, the barrier has greatly reduced suicide bomber attacks since it first began to be built in 2002. The Palestinians, however, see it as a land grab, further picking away at what they continually ask the United Nations to establish as a Palestinian state.

It seems unlikely there is another line or border on the planet that better delineates the world of one culture from that of another.

In the United States, we divide church and state, while at the same time, churchgoers seem to be living in separate worlds when they are at church, at work, or at home. Each has a unique set of rules and governing principles that do not apply to the other. Integrity can mean completely different things in these environments. Each can also have a completely different language—and a completely different tone of voice may also be the rule. This incongruity takes its own toll on our relationships and dreams. It is small thinking that is limiting in so many different ways.

However, Phil also told me another story when we spoke:

When I was in Egypt in April (2011), on the last day we were there, we heard a story about one of the local towns where there had been a lot of interracial violence between the Christians and the Muslims. On this particular day, as the Muslims went to the town square to pray, the Christians followed them. The Christians then held hands in a circle around the Muslims to protect them as they prayed. When the Christians went to church that evening, the Muslims followed them and held hands in a circle around the church to protect the Christians as they prayed.

Now, two things happened on that day in that community. One is they chose a response based on love to a situation very clearly based on fear. The second thing is, their world just got bigger. They said, "OK, we are stepping beyond this thing that divides us that is called religion because we are bigger than this." So their behaviors could evolve to express what is in their hearts rather than what was in their society.

Despite the conflict and hatred we commonly see presented by the news media, stories like this are refreshing examples of how simple and intuitive acts of love can be. Although there is a love and compassion that can overwhelm us to take action, the more challenging thing is "unconditional love." This kind of love we see more rarely. Enduring love is not based on emotion alone; it is an exercise of the will. It takes conscious thought, creativity, and choice.

Certainly such things can become habitual in our lives, but for us to develop the "habit" of acting with unconditional love, we must expand our conscious awareness of what we are doing and change the thoughtless actions that undermine our true purposes. It means expanding our world to include those whom we before saw as our enemies—living in one congruent, authentic world—rather than having a different set of standards for each of the different "realms" of our lives—family, work, worship, with friends, and so forth.

To do this, we must find a way to expand our consciousness—to increase the awareness of each moment in which we live so that we can read the gauges in our mind's control center and let the mini-me of our wills decide how to respond in love rather than from our baser instincts to protect and promote ourselves. Fear and desire for personal pleasure will always take the upper hand until we train ourselves to act in love through repeatedly choosing to do so. Natural patterns of the mind must be overcome with supernatural patterns. One of the definitions of *virtue* is "moral strength," and another is "excellence." To be the virtuous people God has called us to be will demand resolve, building ourselves up in our spirits, and living in the *"still more excellent way"* of love.[1]

I believe that when people connect their aspirations with who they are and what they do, something incredible happens. They begin living their lives authentically, tapping into their potential until they become agents of change—influencing growth, development, and progress within their spheres of influence. When they connect with others, who within their spheres of personal influence are experiencing a similar process, something even more extraordinary happens. They change the way we do life, because their collective contributions to the growth and development of communities and industries ultimately contributes to the advancement of humanity.

Great examples of individuals who epitomize my belief include history makers such as Mohandas Gandhi, Martin Luther King Jr., Sir Winston Churchill, Oprah Winfrey, Michael Jackson, Stephen Jobs, and Walt Disney, among many others. These individuals did not just make history, they shaped it. Their biographies are complex and riddled with challenges in that they are a study of both success and failure. But they each discovered their "why" and now inspire us to do the same. They thought less about "me" and "I" and more about "we" and "us."

You and I, however, cannot do this unless we recognize when we are acting in fear or remaining stuck in the patterns of our past. We must increase our awareness of the moment and be open to feedback both from others and from our consciences. Feedback is a powerful tool if done in the right way. *Wired* magazine recently had an article on the power of even the simplest of feedback loops. Local communities had done everything they could to reduce speeding in school zones—from constant patrols to raising the penalty for tickets to creating more eye-catching speed limit signs—but nothing worked. Then someone happened upon the idea of putting up signs that used radar to show drivers how fast they were driving—giving them instant feedback in bright red numbers. The result? Drivers slowed down immediately after seeing the signs. On average, the signs reduced speed by about 14 percent. There was no penalty, no reprimand from officers, just objective and instant feedback that reminded the person of the speed limit and reflected to them how much over it they were going at the moment. Oddly that same information was openly displayed before them on the speedometers of their cars, but somehow this outside feedback carried more weight.

This same principle has been in practice in Christianity from the beginning. Even though prayer and asking God for forgiveness is all that is required—*"If we confess our sins* [to God], *He is faithful and just to forgive us our sins and to cleanse us from all unrighteousness"*— we are still told to *"confess your sins to one another and pray for one another, that you may be healed."*[2] Solutions come from sharing our mistakes and receiving feedback in nonjudgmental and loving ways. We are also told:

> *Speaking the truth in love, we are to grow up in every way*
> *into Him who is the head, into Christ, from whom the whole*
> *body, joined and held together by every joint with which it is*
> *equipped, when each part is working properly, makes the body*
> *grow so that it builds itself up in love.*[3]

In other words, this level of feedback and accountability—which breeds quality relationships and trust if done properly—will create a culture of growth, love, and virtue building up every individual member as well as the entire body of those joined together in this way. It appears that the more objective and nonjudgmental such feedback is, the better. This feedback, though given in love, is still not easy to take. Facing our own faults and violations of our own values and principles—even for the sake of getting closer to our true purpose— takes a type of courage that is rare. It takes a level of authenticity that is the mark of very few.

Thus we face an odd paradox: the best thing that individuals can do for the world is to be the best, most authentic individual they can be, dedicated to their own personal destiny above that of all others. At the same time, no individual can fulfill their destiny alone or with themselves at the center of their own personal world. Jesus did not simply command us to "love our neighbors" but that first, *"you shall love the Lord your God with all your heart and with all your soul and with all your mind and with all your strength"* and then *"love your neighbor **as yourself**."*[4] In effect, loving others takes us outside of our own personal universe to consider others just as much as we consider ourselves—no more and no less. Loving God opens those small universes even farther to include those who hate us as well as the rest of creation. Through loving God, we also engage with the spiritual—the dimension of possibilities—so that we might be enabled. We open ourselves to be instructed, confronted, and transformed by God through communicating with Him, equipping us to fulfill the destiny He created us to realize.

Though it is every bit miraculous, it is not an overnight process. It happens through a partnership of yielding and growing, studying and praying, loving and pondering. It demands engagement with the spiritual side of ourselves as well as the problems we see in the world. It demands confronting the evil both within ourselves and in the world around us, evaluating where we stand with respect to our values both personally and communally, and tackling the personal and interpersonal discrepancies and inconsistencies that hold us back. We must seek and listen to the feedback that will help us overcome our personal blind spots and allow us to grow and mature to reach our greatest potentials.

To this end, the Barrett Values Centre, founded by former World Bank executive Richard Barrett, has created a survey to measure an organization's, a community's, or a country's current perceived values vis-à-vis their adherence to them. Based on Maslow's hierarchy of needs, the Barrett Centre survey looks for positive and negative values and activities that fall into seven categories.[5] (See Diagram E.) From the bottom up, these are:

1. **Survival:** Is there a sense of financial stability and personal safety? Are health and welfare needs met? Negative aspects of this would be acting with excessive control and caution, exploitation, maintaining only a short-term focus, or rewarding corruption and greed.

2. **Relationships:** Are relationships harmonious enough for everyone to have a sense of belonging and loyalty for both employees and customers? Is interaction based on rivalry or cooperation? Negatives in this category would be using manipulation as a leadership style, rewarding blame, gossip, and allowing discrimination.

3. **Self-esteem:** Are the systems, procedures, and policies built to promote order, quality, and excellence? Are employees trained to high standards, and do they have a sense of pride in their work and the organization? Do supervisors steal ideas and present them as their own? Negative practices that fall under this heading include bureaucracy, overemphasis on hierarchy, teams having a bunker mentality, individual power and status is sought rather than promoting the good of the team and organization, arrogance is rewarded, and there is confusion or a general complacency throughout.

4. **Transformation:** These are the values that transition the organization from impotence to significance. Accountability and responsibility are encouraged while all members have a voice and participate in decision-making, values determination, and goal setting. Innovation, continuous improvement, knowledge sharing, and personal growth are all encouraged.

5. **Internal Cohesion:** The organization has a clear sense of vision, what its values are, and solid communication from top to bottom. Members are enthusiastic, creative, committed, and passionate.

6. **Making a Difference:** The organization has mutually beneficial partnerships and strategic alliances with other organizations and communities. It is environmentally responsible. It also has a strong sense of internal cooperation between departments and divisions.

7. **Service:** The organization is marked by social responsibility that enhances the sustainability of humanity and the planet.

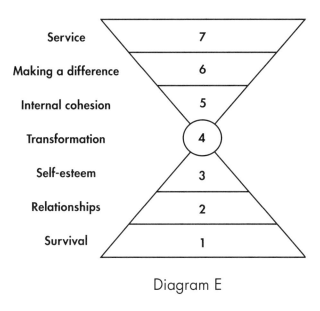

Diagram E

Compassion, humility, and forgiveness are fostered both inside and outside its membership.

Levels one through three focus on the basic needs and viability of the organization and those it serves. These are the basic, somewhat unromantic processes and management issues that make a company profitable, a nonprofit attractive to volunteers and influential in its community, and government services stable and effective. Nor can organizations and nonprofits that fail to adequately address these issues succeed in delivering their mission and vision. They are measures of the organization's virtues as reflected in its competencies and procedures, or its vices as reflected in its poor or hypocritical practices.

Level four is the point of cultural change, transforming fear-based behaviors or deficiencies to more inclusive, adaptive practices that feed empowerment and innovation. When the organization starts to exhibit values like balance, teamwork, participating in continuing education and incremental improvement, and accountability, it is turning the corner to being not only a great place to work but also a difference-maker in its industry and community. This is the level of courage, risk-taking, and challenging the status quo that requires people to step forward and face their fears.

Levels five through seven represent a company that exhibits high values and cohesive alignment. Values are integrated with performance, and the company is equally responsible to employees, clients, and the environment. These companies are wonderful if they also have the core competencies of the first four levels, because pie-in-the-sky values cannot rescue it from an inability to execute as a business. This seems to happen more with nonprofits and non-government organizations (NGOs), where values inspired the formation of the organizations before they had the basic competencies needed to sustain themselves.

Companies and organizations that have and perform according to positive values at all levels also show profit at all three levels of triple-bottom-line evaluation, which takes into consideration the three "P"s—people, the planet, and profit. By broadening the measure for successful business away from a single, financial bottom line, corporations are not only finding ways to create healthier company cultures but are also enhancing their own longevity, image, and sustainability. They may not make as much money in the short term, but they increase their long-term viability, which is ultimately a benefit for themselves and their employees.

The Barrett team asks people to choose from a list of values and practices in response to three different questions:

- **Personal Values:** Participants select ten values/behaviors that most reflect who they are, but not who they desire to become.

- **Current Cultural Values:** Participants select ten values/ behaviors that most reflect how their organization currently operates.

- **Desired Cultural Values:** Participants select the ten values/ behaviors they would like their organization to achieve for peak performance.

These values/behaviors are ones chosen to represent each of the seven levels of organizational consciousness, some of which are positive and some of which are negative. Once the surveys are finished, the Barrett team will determine the top ten for each question and then chart them according to the seven levels. This will give an objective, nutshell evaluation of how the company is performing with respect to its values.[6]

In addition to this, negative behaviors and values feed into what is called the "cultural entropy" factor. In other words, how much time does the organization waste on activities that are counterproductive? Examples of these would be too much bureaucracy, rewarding those who blame others rather than those who take responsibility, aversion to risk, inefficiency, short-term thinking and planning, complacency, and so forth. This is then turned into a percentage to illustrate just how much of a business's time and focus is lost to negative activity and energy. Companies that have less than 10 percent cultural entropy are doing pretty well; those with more than 40 percent are likely to fail, implode, or go bankrupt soon.

No one sets out to create a company that is a toxic place to work or poisonous to the planet, just as no one marries looking to divorce or has children hoping to raise delinquents or criminals. The problem is that we focus on the wrong measurements or else behave in unhealthy ways without ever realizing it. In the Barrett Model, entropy activities very rarely show up on the personal or desired values; they are primarily in the current culture values. In other words, it is the disconnection between values and performance that undermines our cultures, whether in the home, in the organization, or in the community.

The Barrett Leadership Model trains individuals to lead themselves first, then teams, then organizations, and then society. This transformational process to becoming an effective agent of change must start with an inner discovery of purpose and values. It begins with healing one's own soul, as we discussed in Part 1 of this book. Until that process is undertaken, attempts to create outer transformation in relationships, teams, organizations, or communities will be fruitless.

We must first lead ourselves, being aware of what we are doing and why, free of past fears and stumbling blocks, so that we can push on to be the leaders God has called each of us to be.

The fact of the matter is that businesses are good for the world, and business executives are smart, capable people. They have an incredible ability to accomplish what they set out to accomplish. As business guru Peter Drucker is famously credited with saying, "What gets measured gets done." But as leadership expert and motivational speaker Bob Harrison commonly says, "Setting goals can be the most dangerous thing you do. Because once you set a goal in one area, you've just excluded all others." If all we measure is the bottom line of profit and all of our energies are focused on improving that one number, then it shouldn't be surprising that other concerns that are just as important, if not more important, are somehow overlooked. Because areas like our impact on the environment, our company cultures, and our values are less tangible and more difficult to measure, they too often get neglected.

Things like Barrett's seven levels of organizational conscious-ness and the triple bottom line evaluation methodology create new paradigms for how we organize business and measure success. Such measurement systems demand that we ask more holistic, inclusive questions in order to create more holistic, inclusive organizations. They are game-changers and paradigm-shifters. From them, we begin to realize we should prize cooperation over competition, both internally and externally, because that is the most sustainable methodology. They create new paradigms that change the size of the world of each leader and each member of the organization. It changes the emphasis from being the best *in* the world to being the best *for* the world, and our worlds also grow larger and more congruent as a result.

We don't live one way at home, another at church, and a completely different way in the workplace. We find balance and integrity living one life, not several. Happy home lives become just as prized as meeting deadlines. Relationships become a higher priority in the workplace, enhancing both our personal and professional lives. We learn to make do with "enough" rather than gouging employees or clients to increase our profit margins—while investing whatever is "more than enough" in the self-actualization of others, whether they be our colleagues, our clients, our competitors, our families, or people in the developing world.

An outstanding example of the power of triple bottom line evaluation is the work of the Savory Institute. The organization's founder, Allan Savory, was born and grew up in Rhodesia (Zambia and Zimbabwe today) in southern Africa. He started as a research biologist and game ranger, and later went on to become a farmer, game rancher, politician, and international consultant. Faced with the interrelated problems of increasing poverty and disappearing wildlife in the 1960s, he realized that the desertification and degradation of the world's grassland ecosystems was a central issue that affected multiple problems. Through study, trial and error (the final significant pieces of the puzzle not falling into place until the 1980s), and observing the natural patterns of this ecosystem as an integrated whole, he discovered that by grazing cattle or other such large herbivores in ways that mimicked the natural migration of wild herds in predator/prey environments, grasslands did not become more barren, but rather more fertile.

Where burning fields or letting them sit dormant for years did little, grazing them as he prescribed revitalized not only the plant life, but also the wildlife. Species that had long been absent returned in numbers, and deserts were turned into life-sustaining prairies. Not only that, but the process took only a handful of years, rather than decades. As a result, lands that have been without water for over a hundred years are now home to thriving wetlands with no fear of drought or famine. The increased vitality of these grasslands also absorbs carbon from the atmosphere in large quantities, greatly reducing one of the main contributors to global warming. In fact, Mr. Savory has spoken repeatedly at the United Nations and stated that even if we stopped all the carbon emissions being put into the atmosphere today, it wouldn't be enough to reverse the trend—and would only be a drop in the bucket compared to what revitalizing of the world's grasslands would do.[7] Today, the Savory Method is being introduced around the world with great success, even though the work that needs to done has only just begun.

The Savory Institute has also put together a decision-making process that could have significant application for other land management enterprises and businesses. Their research is fascinating on many levels, and not just for those reasons already mentioned. As a business model, it seems to have only a few peers at the moment—although every measure of the triple bottom line is improved; Savory's "Holistic Management" revitalizes overgrazed or degraded lands previously seen as barren and useless, producing healthier, grass-fed animals that go for premium prices in the marketplaces. In poorer countries, this increases the quantity of healthy, nutritious meat, decreasing both hunger and malnutrition. It has a similar revitalizing effect for dairies and sheep raised to produce wool. Local ranchers, farmers, and herders make better profits, and those profits get fed back into local economies. As a result, demand increases in these areas for other goods and services. It is capitalism at its best!

While some in the third world are pointing to free market capitalism as a failed system, it is still the best model for encouraging both individuals and organizations to reach their potentials. The answer is not in changing the system so much as it is in enlarging our worlds and changing the way we measure success. The self-interest of Adam Smith's "invisible hand" was not one that was supposed to endorse the actions of the greedy and corrupt but to show, in the end, that such actions would eventually bring companies to failure and national economies to their knees, just as we have seen in the last decade. "Free market" activity would have allowed those exercising poor practices to fail. Unfortunately that would have cost too many too much—especially investors and clients. While the bailouts of Wall Street and failed European economies are the right thing to do on a humanitarian level, we don't want to send the wrong messages either. We cannot endorse the practices that caused the crises in the first place.

Ultimately, we need a new brand of leader who has a more inclusive worldview. We need people to step to the helm of organizations, businesses, and governments who will not be ruled by their distorted egos or motivated solely by the bottom line and how much they can eke out for themselves. The world is in crisis for the lack of such leaders. It is time for us to step forward and become those leaders, whether we have the authority written into our job descriptions or not.[8]

> *"Leadership" is a concept we often resist...But if it is true that we are part of a community, then leadership is everyone's vocation, and it can be an evasion to insist that it is not. When we live in the close-knit ecosystem called community, everyone follows and everyone leads.... It's out of the ferment of community that real change comes.*
>
> —PARKER PALMER, *LET YOUR LIFE SPEAK*

> *Leadership is the scarcest resource, and the most important resource, in the world. Nothing happens without leadership.*
>
> —ROBERT MCDONALD

History maker arise...from "I" to "us" without "them."

Consider and then arise to answer: How hard would it be for you to expand your world to include those you see as enemies—*"them"*? How possible is it to think about living in one compatible, authentic world rather than in a world where you assign different standards and worth to different people? And how much of a paradigm shift would it take for you to value cooperation over competition, compassion over me-first?

Beginning with you and then expanding to include family, colleagues, etc., can you exchange being the best *in* the world to being the best *for* the world? As your worlds grow with these principles in place, the more compatible each will be.

You will find balance and integrity living one life, not several. When relationships at home, at church, and at work become a higher priority than fierce competitiveness, you will make do with "enough." In assisting with the self-actualization of others, true purpose comes from an I/us perspective, with "them" included in "we."

History maker arise...to pray for your enemies.

Heavenly Father, I open myself to Your unconditional love so that I can share that love with others, including those who dislike me, hold grudges, or otherwise are averse to me. Please expand my small universe to include the spiritual dimension of possibilities where You can instruct, confront, and transform me.

Dear Lord, partnering with You means focusing more on You and "them" than on "me" and "I." When teamed with You, my spiritual eyes are opened to see the problems in the world—and in me. You, God, can help me evaluate and tackle the personal and interpersonal inconsistencies and conflicts that hold me back from growing and maturing into the person who appreciates and loves all people who come alongside me— thus shaping history in a very good way. So be it.

CHAPTER TEN

being a leader/follower

The words of the wise heard in quiet are better than the shouting of a ruler among fools. Wisdom is better than weapons of war, but one sinner destroys much good.

—ECCLESIASTES 9:17–18

All labor that uplifts humanity has dignity and importance, and should be undertaken with painstaking excellence.

—DR. MARTIN LUTHER KING JR.

King Solomon tells a great story in the Book of Ecclesiastes that has long fascinated me. A small village is surrounded by the army of a great king. Siegeworks have been built, and the troops are prepared to scale the walls and plunder the town. As the villagers cower in fear of what is about to happen, a poor beggar steps forward with a plan. Through his wisdom, the attacking army is defeated and the village is saved.

Solomon goes on to comment, though, that despite all that he had done for the city, because the man was poor, no one remembered him.[1] Even though wisdom is better than might, we tend to care more about who the messenger is than what the message is. We are more interested in who gets the credit than that the innovation happens. This is a failure of culture and a failure of leadership.

What if that village had rejected that poor man's advice because he was only a lowly member of the community rather than a leader? Then the village would have been lost. Do our organizations and businesses suffer from the same narrow-mindedness today?

Too often individuals, businesses, or organizations fail to prosper because of an idea they haven't had yet, never recognized as important, or gave up on too quickly. We miss transformational ideas because they are outside of our worldview or come from a source we do not esteem. When everyone is concerned about who gets credit for the latest breakthrough, implementing the right idea becomes more a process of political influence and posturing than evaluating what is truly best for the organization. A leader who can't listen to every voice in his organization, regardless of the person's position or authority, isn't interested in leading as much as being in control.

There is a huge difference between leading and managing— leaders inspire and empower for the benefit of all; managers organize and delegate to get jobs done. The two characteristics can be in the same person, but for that person to be successful, she or he will need to understand when to let which role come to the forefront. A great leader will also know when it is best to follow someone else for the good of all, while those hungry for power will cut the very foundation out from under their own organization to stay in charge or to extract more financial reward for themselves.

We have certainly seen this kind of leadership failure in the financial sector in recent years, both in the United States and in Europe. Being too shortsighted and focusing only on the bottom line encouraged the creation of risky investments and dubious trading tactics that eventually cost many dearly. Again, it is not that people were dishonest or incompetent but that they were somehow engrossed with the wrong things. As former Harvard Business School professor Dr. Shoshana Zuboff put it:

> I spent a quarter century as a professor at the Harvard Business School, including fifteen years teaching in the MBA program. I have come to believe that much of what my colleagues and I taught has caused real suffering, suppressed wealth creation, destabilized the world economy, and accelerated the demise of the twentieth-century capitalism in which the U.S. played the leading role.
>
> We weren't stupid and we weren't evil. Nevertheless we managed to produce a generation of managers and business professionals that is deeply mistrusted and despised by a majority of people in our society and around the world. This is a terrible failure.[2]

Echoing this sentiment, Michael Jacobs, a professor at the University of North Carolina's Kenan-Flagler Business School, wrote the following for the *Wall Street Journal*:

> By failing to teach the principles of corporate governance, our business schools have failed our students. And by not internalizing sound principles of governance and accountability, business school graduates have matured into executives and investment bankers who have failed American workers, and retirees who have witnessed their jobs and savings vanish....
>
> Could we have avoided most of the economic problems we now face if we had a generation of business leaders who were trained in designing compensation systems that promote long-term value? And who were educated in the proper makeup and responsibilities of boards? And who were enlightened as to how shareholders can use their proxies to affect accountability? I think we could have.

America's business schools need to rethink what we are teaching—and not teaching—the next generation of leaders.[3]

When leaders are basically incentivized to do what is bad for their businesses in the long run, as well as bad for their national economies, it is hard to hold them solely accountable when they fail. They were operating out of a wrong paradigm. They were shortsighted because they were never taught to think long-term and planet-wide—or about how fragile the house of cards was that they were building. They thought they were doing what was best for their industry, even if they were stepping wholeheartedly into dark gray areas of business ethics, because they were "succeeding" according to the measures they were using. Would they have done differently had their evaluation systems been more holistic? I have to think they would have.

The world needs an awakening to a new kind of leadership—what I like to call being a leader/follower.

Many have tried to communicate this idea through the concept of servant leadership, but I think that term is too easily dismissed or misinterpreted. Most, if not all, corporate leaders have little understanding of what it means to be a servant to others and will even pat themselves on the back for being servant leaders—even as they abuse their own employees and work through manipulation rather than influence. Meanwhile, others are too good at the servant role and get lost as people steal their ideas and the credit for their work. True leaders cannot be those blinded by either their own bloated opinions of themselves or their desperate need to receive approval and recognition. If they are, they lack the authenticity to effectively choose the best path forward and will instead get bogged down in their own soulish shortcomings. Achieving your goals is great—unless they are bad goals or are measured by the wrong criteria. And again, I believe that is exactly what happened in the United States in 2008 with the housing crisis.

That's why I prefer the concept of a leader/follower to that of a servant leader, though for all intents and purposes the description of each is very similar. The leader/follower, however, won't be as concerned about title and job description before they act. As a supervisor, the leader/follower will be someone who can get the most out of their team and allow every voice to be heard. The authentic leader/follower will know when to take the helm and when to follow the ideas of others—or let someone else take the lead in a particular area or on a project. Only someone operating as an effective leader/follower can be an effective delegator, neither micromanaging nor ineffectively communicating expectations and goals.

It's not unusual to see companies and organizations whose growth stalls because their founder/president does not sufficiently trust his or her coworkers to do their jobs. Leaders who can't truly let go of aspects of management placed into the hands of others will continually meddle in them, taking up valuable time for themselves and the subordinate in asking too many questions or getting involved in too many minor details. A codependent leader will even interfere without realizing it, making arbitrary changes just for the sake of asserting authority. They want to feel as if they have a voice in decision-making, even if it undermines pre-established chains of communication and command. Imagine how limiting it is, for example, when the leader has to take part in every conversation that goes on in the company—even those of minor importance!

By contrast, look at companies known to be innovators and how their conversations flow. At Apple, when renovating their buildings, Steve Jobs had walls torn down and bathrooms moved to change traffic patterns so interdepartmental conversations would happen in passing. Because of this, on the chance of seeing someone who had been talking about something at the last meeting, the memory would be jogged and a relevant point might be shared that wouldn't have otherwise. This intentional spontaneous interaction helped spur ideas that needed other ideas to succeed—more chances for ideas to collide created more opportunities for innovations to emerge. Imagine how different that is than an office where everything has to go through several layers of supervisors or where interdepartmental communications are closely controlled.

At the other extreme, a person doesn't have to be a supervisor to be a leader/follower. A person can, in effect, lead from the bottom by being a conscientious worker who is not afraid to speak up when the time is right. Motivational speaker Brian Tracy encourages people to think of themselves as CEO of their own organization no matter what they do—for even if they are the only one they supervised, they need to conduct themselves as an army of one.

Leader/followers at this level can also assert influence by being the best followers they can be and having the same broad worldview that would make a good company president or chairman of the board.

Leader/followers must be anchored by their values as much as they are driven by their ambitions. The "rules of the game" in any organization should reflect its long-term values rather than reinforce hierarchy and authoritarianism. Good manners are the oil that lubricates relationships and cooperation—they are practiced to help people work together more efficiently and more joyfully, not just because that's the way our parents taught us to behave. We don't "play fair" because cheating is wrong but because in the long run, those who play fair win together. Policies and procedures can thus change as needed to reflect changing times or attitudes, but values will stay the same. We live in rapidly shifting times—if our organizations can't adapt, they will fail. Remembering and dialoguing about our values, however, will help us keep first things first as we adapt so that changes don't, in the end, change what we are really about.

According to the research of Rosabeth Moss Kanter, a professor at Harvard Business School and chairperson of the Harvard University Advanced Leadership Initiative, companies that have widespread discussion of their values are actually more innovative, profitable, and responsible because such discussions enhance accountability, collaboration, and initiative.[4]

There is a balance that must be struck between the needs and contribution of each individual and that of the group overall. As the old adage goes, "If everyone thinks alike, someone is not thinking."

While discussion and interaction are important, it is almost always individuals who have the breakthrough ideas or come up with the breakthrough product. The culture is important to feed individual needs and create an environment for creativity and productivity, while it is individuals who do the work and come up with the ideas that make the culture prosperous. It gives a whole new perspective to how Paul saw the Church as a body belonging to every member of it:

> For the body does not consist of one member but of many. If the foot should say, "Because I am not a hand, I do not belong to the body," that would not make it any less a part of the body. And if the ear should say, "Because I am not an eye, I do not belong to the body," that would not make it any less a part of the body. If the whole body were an eye, where would be the sense of hearing? If the whole body were an ear, where would be the sense of smell? But as it is, God arranged the members in the body, each one of them, as he chose. If all were a single member, where would the body be?[5]

Without our diversity, we would be blind in one area or another; without our unity, we would be unable to compensate for those blind spots. Inability to organize is a barrier to not only success, but also survival. Those who would be leader/followers will not only recognize this, but they will also nurture it—whether they are the CEO or someone in IT.

Such a leader will be described very much like how Kanter described the chairman and CEO of PepsiCo, Indra Nooyi, as an example of what she saw as the leader of the future:

> In the face of turbulence and change, culture and values become the major source of continuity and coherence, of renewal and sustainability. Leaders must be institution-builders who imbue the organization with meaning that inspires today and endures tomorrow. They must find an underlying purpose and a strong set of values that serve as a basis for longer-term decisions even in the midst of

volatility. They must find the common purpose and universal values that unite highly diverse people while still permitting individual identities to be expressed and enhanced. Indeed, emphasizing purpose and values helps leaders support and facilitate self-organizing networks that can respond quickly to change because they share an understanding of the right thing to do.[6]

Dutch-born Tex Gunning, former president of Unilever Asia, adds depth to the demands and character of the leaders our planet's future will need:

Average leaders take care of themselves and their families. Good leaders take care of themselves, their families, and some of the community. Great leaders—and great companies—not only take care of these stakeholders, but also want to change the world. They want to leave the world better than they found it. We have made the choice to have our business intent become a missionary intent that will make a difference in the lives of Asians who have either health problems, nutritional problems, or wellbeing problems.[7]

The core insight about great leadership and great companies comes down to service. We as individuals should entirely integrate our personal lives and our search for meaning with our business lives. Businesses with a meaningful intent will bring meaning to the lives of their employees. Then it will be as if we were volunteers—paid volunteers—in a community service organization. And we'll only need half the policies, half the training, half the values statements that are usually needed in business because people will be living out their deepest values everywhere in their lives.

According to Richard Barrett, the leaders of the future will need traits that can be summarized in three points:

1. They will have a worldview that counts the global society as part of "us";

2. They will create companies that are resilient over time because they are anchored and motivated by values, rather than policies and practices, and therefore have more holistic measurements of success; and

3. Their companies will be nimble and adaptable to changes in an increasingly fluctuating world market.[8]

In brief, such leaders exhibit emotional intelligence, the ability to put off short-term gratification for long-term benefit. They are willing to put in the work and pay the price now that will pay dividends in the future, whether that means dieting and exercise for long-term health on the personal front or building a sounder though costlier infrastructure so that the company can be more environmentally responsible down the road. Such leaders don't shy away from doing what is right in lieu of doing what is expedient.

On a day-in, day-out level, however, this can be a tough stance to take. It means fighting for what is right when others don't see it. It could mean taking financial losses for a time or a lower initial salary for long-term environmental and social benefits. It means understanding what is enough, building assets rather than continually operating on credit, growing a little more slowly, and welcoming innovation *wherever* it might come from. Such a leader will certainly be marked by the fruit of the Spirit described in Galatians 5:22–23—love, joy, peace, patience, kindness, goodness, faithfulness, gentleness, and self-control. Barrett characterizes these a little differently. He says these leaders will be marked and guided by:

- **Altruism:** The ability to devote yourself to meeting the needs of others by making their concerns central to your life.

- **Humor:** The ability to make fun of your situation and thereby lighten the load of what you have to bear.

- **Suppression:** The ability to postpone paying attention to an impulse or conflict until you are calm enough to deal with it.

- **Anticipation:** The ability to anticipate and plan for the possibility of future inner discomfort and manage the process.

- **Sublimation:** The ability to attenuate or channel the expression of instinctual responses into avenues of expression that do not result in adverse consequences for yourself or others.[9]

While those who are less adept will use strategies such as the following to handle conflict and stress:

- **Repression:** Blocking conscious perception of feelings and instincts.

- **Passive-aggressive behavior:** Sublimated aggression expressed indirectly by passivity.

- **Projection:** Relieving unacknowledged pain by projecting feelings onto others.

- **Intellectualization:** Denying the feelings being experienced by rationalizing the situation away.

- **Acting out:** Engaging in tantrums and motor impulses to avoid dealing with tension and one's own feelings.[10]

Are you seeing the pattern here? The same skills and awareness needed to be a healthy, balanced, thriving soul are the foundation of being a healthy, balanced, thriving leader! Certainly that is not all there is to it, but it should be evident that as we learn the nuts and bolts of business and leadership—or any other endeavor, for that matter—to neglect prospering our souls is to not only handicap us but to potentially make us leaders to disaster and crisis rather than environmental, cultural, and economic sustainability. How do I know? Because that is where soulless leadership has guided us to date.

So my questions to you are: "Where will such soul-healthy leaders come from? Where will we learn to prosper our souls?" If it's not being learned in the business schools, if it's not being taught in our technical colleges, if it's not being developed in our economics and financial leaders of the future, and if it's not being passed on through our law schools and to our political science and international relations majors, where are the innovators of the future going to learn to become people who are healthy in spirit, soul, and body so that they might have the broadest vision for making the best world possible for tomorrow?

I believe it has to start in our communities of faith and move from there into our everyday workplaces. We must release our understanding of spiritual things from our houses of faith and into our communities in non-toxic ways. To do that, we need to learn to ask tougher questions in our faith communities and better understand how to cultivate and nurture innovation from our spiritual selves.

I believe the kind of leader we are looking for is the one staring back at you when you look in the mirror. Your authentic self is the divine seed of potential God put inside you—the deposit God made when He formed you. You are purpose-built. Dare to be you and place all your efforts into being the best you that you can be. As Ralph Waldo Emerson said, "To be yourself in a world that is constantly trying to make you something else is the greatest accomplishment."[11]

You are built for greatness. To distinguish yourself among the great, you must get off the sidelines and get in the game of life. "Whatever course you decide upon," Emerson continued, "there is always someone to tell you that you are wrong. There are always difficulties arising which tempt you to believe that your critics are right. To map out a course of action and follow it to an end requires courage."[12]

To change a situation, we must first change ourselves—most especially our perception of ourselves. Just as the saying "hurting people hurt people" is true, healthy people can help heal others and ultimately our world.

The link between healing and living authentically is to know who you have been created to be and to fulfill your life purpose with passion. Whatever most grips your heart is the mystery God has set before you to unlock. By unveiling the innovation that God has hidden within your own soul, you become the answer the world—or someone in it—is looking for. It is your destiny, and only you can fulfill it—and be fulfilled by it.

> *If your actions create a legacy that inspires*
> *others to dream more, learn more, do more and*
> *become more, then, you are an excellent leader.*
>
> —DOLLY PARTON

History maker arise...to your call as a leader/follower.

The world needs you to fulfill your role as a leader/follower. As such, you respect every voice yearning to be heard and know when someone else's ideas are most useful. You know when to take the lead and when another is more capable in certain arenas. Effectively communicating expectations and goals provides the balance between the needs and contributions of each individual as well as the group as a whole. Your emotional intelligence will be welcomed as followers realize the benefits of postponing short-term gratification for long-term dividends. You will do what is right rather than cutting corners.

Does this describe you now or in the not-too-distant future? Whether the leader of a business, organization, ministry, community group, family, or a party of one, your role as a leader/follower is important to a wider audience than you may ever realize. Devote yourself to manifesting the qualities of a leader/follower in the coming days, especially focusing on altruism, humor, self-control, forward thinking, and tuning into the whispers of God in your ear.

History maker arise...in prayer for soul-healthy leaders.

The Creator knows that the world lacks soul-healthy leaders. When we neglect prospering our souls, we lose sight of the spiritual realm where most of reality resides. Of course we pray for our "daily bread," but we must not abandon the larger, looming environmental, cultural, social, political, and economic leadership issues.

So, Lord God, I pray that You will prosper my soul through Your Word, the Bible, through people You place in my life, through the example of Your Son Jesus Christ, and through the gift of the Holy Spirit living in me—urging me to become healthy in spirit, soul, and body so I can step into a leader/follower role and broaden my vision for making the best world possible for tomorrow and many tomorrows to follow—shaping history to reflect the very best of You. Amen.

CHAPTER ELEVEN

the anatomy of innovation

*If I were to wish for anything, I should not wish for wealth
and power, but for the passionate sense of the potential,
for the eye which ever young and ardent, sees the possible.
Pleasure disappoints, possibility never.*

—SØREN KIERKEGAARD, *EITHER / OR*

*Genius happens at this place where your values and your
strengths intersect and engage in tandem....When your
values lead, your best, most rewarding work follows.*

—GINA RUDAN, *FIVE STEPS TO PRACTICAL GENIUS*

I am sure you have heard it said, "Necessity is the mother of invention," but I don't believe that is exactly true. At best, necessity is the father of invention, giving the seed of an idea that is nurtured to fruition in the imagination and the mind. I believe the true mother of invention and innovation is the soul.

As the intermediary between the physical and the spiritual—between the realms of the practical and the possible, the natural and the supernatural—the soul is the fertile soil into which ideas are planted and then nurtured and cultivated into reality. Ideas—artistic, technological, social, political, or theoretical—are the beginning place of all innovation, but they are only seeds. Sometimes the plants turn out quite differently than how we originally envisioned they would because they take on the nutrients or toxins they find in the soil. That is how a seemingly good idea, like deregulated financial trading, can turn out so poorly in actuality. Because of their failure to recognize the nature of individuals caught between ambition and selfishness and their failure to mediate, cultures run amok when greed is not curbed; great ideas turn to colossal disasters if we fail to judge them by their effects on society and the environment as well as the personal pocketbook.

We see a similar thing happen just a generation or so after Noah's ark settled on Mount Ararat. Humanity shared a common language and lived primarily in one culture in the Middle East. Bound together in purpose and need, innovations were rapidly made in building techniques and agricultural practices. Cities formed and individuals applied themselves to solving the problems caused by great numbers of people living in the same area, such as the need for waste disposal, access to food and water, transportation, textiles, communications, recording history, commerce, medicine, lighting homes, and personal hygiene. As people lived more in communities rather than as wandering hunter-gatherers, innovation happened more rapidly because ideas collided more frequently with other ideas, often finding the companion thoughts or inventions needed to complete themselves. Cities prospered and the population boomed.

The trouble was, in the same way that good ideas can flourish for the good of all, so bad ideas can poison all. It occurred to city leaders that while things were "good," they would be even better if they could build their own stairway to Heaven. They began the construction of a great tower that would rule over all of the earth, and with it they formed their own religion apart from divine influence. With this first form of atheistic humanism came the imminent disaster that would be the Tower of Babel. Unified, humanity would build a tower to reach the heavens, an enterprise not only doomed to failure because of the poor understanding of the nature of the universe—but one that would doom generations of human beings to slavery and a false religion.

Looking down, God saw where things were headed and decided to intervene. Rather than letting generations be lost in the greatest example of the dangers of groupthink the world had yet experienced, He divided them into people groups, races, and languages, forcing them to disperse and populate the earth as He originally intended. He also recognized the potential human beings possessed because of the divine creative spark He had place within them—that part that mirrored His own creative nature.

> *And the Lord said, "Behold, they are one people, and they have all one language, and this is only the beginning of what they will do. And nothing that they propose to do will now be impossible for them."*[1]

God wasn't taking a stance against human creativity here, but He didn't want to see a form of creativity emerge that would ultimately be self-destructive. At the time, there was no other way for human beings to come to God except through individually "running into" Him in the wilderness as it appears Job and Abraham did. God had no voices or prophets on the earth yet to speak for Him, teaching His ways and how to know Him.

Since then, however, things have changed. Human beings have the choice of seeking God or doing their own thing, for God's covenants are on the earth and His voice is heard—though we are filters that are far from perfect in translating His message most of the time. We need to realize it matters where our hearts are—it matters how nutritious and toxin-free our soul is.[2] We must realize that invention, building businesses and nonprofits, as well as seeking to govern justly and intelligently are as much an act of worship as singing on Sunday morning, if not more so. As such, our reaching out into our communities and world should look like much more than membership or pledge drives. We have access to the most creative mind in the universe—that of the Creator Himself!

However, this isn't magic. It's not like you can wave a wand, speak something in Latin, and the innovation the world needs will just appear. The Scriptures tell us, *"It is the glory of God to conceal things, but the glory of kings is to search things out."*[3]

I have heard science described as "the thinking of God's thoughts after Him." I sincerely believe that part of the adventure of pursuing and coming to know God is also to understand the way He created the universe, how it operates, and what we can create after Him from the principles of creation. After all, as Solomon so wisely said, *"There is nothing new under the sun,"* although there are new ways of combining things that others have never considered before.[4] It is our ability to look into the world and make new connections between things that already exist that paves the way to innovation.

Take, for example, Gutenberg's printing press, arguably the most transformational invention the world has ever known. Gutenberg's press not only made the Bible available to the common person but facilitated the dispersion of all other knowledge as well. In the next century, the world experienced the end of the Dark Ages, the Renaissance, the Reformation, the Scientific Revolution, and within approximately a century and a half, the plays of Shakespeare and the King James Bible. And yet nothing that went into making the printing press was original with Gutenberg.

The screw press, which was the main structure of the press, had been in use for pressing grapes to make wine since the time of the Romans. Movable type had been independently developed more than four centuries before by a Chinese blacksmith named Pi Sheng. It never really caught on, however, because it used hand rubbing, which made it roughly as time consuming as transcribing; it offered no real advancement. Paper and ink were already widely used by the publishing industry of that day—scribes sitting at tables hand-copying text from one book into what would become the next.[5]

The revolution came when the metallurgist Gutenberg put all of these pre-existing elements into one device. Suddenly, printing numerous copies of the same book could be done in days instead of months. Printing with Gutenberg's press far surpassed the productivity and accuracy of hand transcription. Books became cheaper, more accessible, and more widely distributed. Old knowledge and new ideas collided more often with hungry minds, and Europe experienced one of the profoundest times of change in history.

But for new ideas to interact with the old ones, we have to be seekers of new experiences and new thoughts! We have to be ponderers of issues that need solutions so that when we meet a new idea that has an element of knowledge that we either didn't know or hadn't put together with what we were contemplating, we can make the connection that provides the solution. As the author of *Creative Thinkering*, Michael Michalko, puts it:

Every individual has the ability to create ideas based on his or her existing patterns of thinking, which are based on education and experience. But without any provision for variations, ideas eventually stagnate and lose their adaptive advantages. In the end, if you always think the way you've always thought, you'll always get what you've always got. The same old ideas.[6]

Breakthrough only comes from change, whether it is a change in behavior, in habit, in environment, or in thinking. Breakthrough comes through the interaction of ideas that have never been put into the same train of thought before—at least for the discovering individual. After all, as we have already discussed, ideas have consequences. We need more permeable worldviews so that the complementary ideas we need to complete one another can slip in and interact. As poet and musician Leonard Cohen put it in his song, "Anthem":

There is a crack, a crack in everything
That's how the light gets in.[7]

Too often, however, we arrive at work, attend school, or go to church starting as question marks and leaving as periods. We enter with questions and leave with statements that are a little more than excuses to maintain the status quo. This is good to an extent, because stability provides a comfort level for everyone and chaos is tough to live with. However, there should be more of a balance—there will be no new creative ideas if there isn't just a little bit of chaos, just as there will be no growth without the discomfort of interacting with new people and paradigms.

Inventors, scientists, and other innovators are people of routine and perseverance, but they are also people who read widely, seek new experiences and new theories, and question everything. They understand the black-and-white nature of truth—the 0 or 1 binary language of computers, for instance—but are also intrigued by the rainbow spectral nature of truth as well, which allows for broader understanding. It is like the old parable of the blind men and the elephant:

> Once upon a time, there lived six blind men in a village. One day the villagers told them, "Hey, there is an elephant in the village today."
>
> They had no idea what an elephant was, so they decided, "Even though we would not be able to see it, let us go and feel it anyway." All of them went to the elephant. Each found a place where they could investigate the elephant using their sense of touch.
>
> The first said, "The elephant is a pillar," because he found one of its legs.
>
> The second, who touched the tail, said, "Oh, no! It is like a rope."
>
> "Oh, no! It is like a thick branch of a tree," said the third man who touched the trunk of the elephant.
>
> "You are all crazy! It is like a big hand fan," said the fourth man who touched the elephant's ear.
>
> "You are all mistaken. An elephant is like a huge wall," said the fifth man, who touched the side of the elephant.

The sixth said, "No, it is like a solid pipe," because he had touched the tusk of the elephant.

They began to argue. Each insisted he was right. It looked like the argument might soon come to blows.

Luckily a wise man happened by. He stopped and asked them, "What is the matter?"

They said, "We cannot agree about what the elephant is like." Then each told the wise man his perspective.

After hearing them out, with a smile, he explained. "Do you not realize that each one of you could be right at the same time? The reason you have different stories is because each one of you touched a different part of the elephant. So, actually the elephant has all those features you described."

After the wise man's explanation, there was no more squabbling. They were happy that they were all correct, but also that they could learn from each other what they would never have learned all by themselves.

As Michalko explains, "Creativity in all domains...emerges from the basic mental operation of conceptual blending of dissimilar subjects. When analyzed, creative ideas are always new combinations of old ideas."[8] There is, indeed, nothing new under the sun, but there are new ways of combining and blending what is under the sun, and that is how breakthroughs happen.

However, it generally takes time for the ideas that need to blend into an innovation or discovery to find each other. Sometimes those ideas don't find each other in time. In his book *Where Good Ideas Come From*, Steven Johnson discusses the story of the famous "Phoenix memo" that Arizona-based FBI agent Ken Williams sent to his superiors as an "electronic communication" on July 10, 2001. In it, Williams put into writing a growing hunch that he'd had:

The purpose of this communication is to advise the Bureau and New York of the possibility of a coordinated effort by USAMA BIN LADEN (UBL) to send students to the United States to attend civil aviation universities and colleges.[9]

Williams believed that Bin Laden was interested in slowly infiltrating the civil aviation industry with the hope of quietly carrying out disruptive acts of terrorism to weaken economies and cause fear. Williams wanted the Bureau to compile a list of aviation institutions in the United States and begin flagging anyone attempting to obtain a visa in order to attend one of these schools. It was a long process and seemed to be almost immediately shelved by anyone who read it. Two months later, when passenger airliners were crashed into the World Trade Center and the Pentagon and another into the Pennsylvanian countryside, Williams's memo became a stabbing rebuke at the inefficiency of the Bureau.

However, had Williams's "slow hunch" connected with another hunch, things might have been different. About a month after Williams submitted his memo, Zacarias Moussaoui enrolled at the Pan Am International Flight Academy near St. Paul, Minnesota, where he began training on a Boeing 747-400 flight simulator. Moussaoui paid his full tuition—$8,300—in cash and then, throughout his training, only really seemed to care about how the cockpit doors and flight communications operated, not things the instructors felt were more important like taking off and landing the plane. Both peaked instructor's curiosity, to say the least. When he later stated he had no real interest in ever flying, someone flagged the front office about his behavior. The school contacted the FBI, and Moussaoui was arrested after a background check found that he was in the country illegally.

During questioning, FBI field agents Harry Samit and Greg Jones got the impression that there was more going on than simply immigration issues and that Moussaoui might be part of a larger conspiracy and active threat. They sought a warrant to examine the files on Moussaoui's laptop, but the request was denied on August 21, 2001, because their grounds for probable cause were deemed "shaky." In asking again, Agent Jones alleged that Moussaoui or someone connected to him might "try to fly something into the World Trade Center."[10] The search warrant was not granted until the afternoon of September 11. When it was finally examined, it was discovered that Moussaoui had direct connections to eleven of the nineteen 9/11 hijackers.

While it is certainly no sure thing that the attacks of September 11 would have been prevented had the FBI gained access to Moussaoui's laptop when they first asked in August, had these two ideas found each other, it seems likely the warrant would have been granted the first time and connections potentially made before the disaster. If it had been, it seems very possible that the Al Qaeda conspiracy to attack the World Trade Center and the Pentagon could have been discovered in time for the FBI to act, detain most of the future hijackers, and cripple bin Laden's plan.

How differently might the last decade have been had these ideas found one another and this plot been foiled? How many would be alive today who are not because of September 11, not just in the towers but around the world? How much more stable would the US economy be without the debt of wars in Iraq and Afghanistan? How different would things be with Iran's nuclear program because it would have been a major focus instead of a sideline show? How different would things be between Israelis and Palestinians because the face of world terrorism would be completely different? There is no way to really know, but it certainly seems like they would be far better had the attacks of 9/11 been prevented.

The thing is, there is no way to estimate the value of an idea or the power of two complementary "hunches" finding each other. If God is active in the world today, He must work His will in this way—for He has legally given authority of the earth to humanity, and He cannot step in if we don't ask. If we would diligently seek His guidance, He will use us to be world changers through the ideas He gives us—the spiritual intuition formed within us to help us understand what is important to pay attention to each day and what is not—and to connect with others who have the ideas necessary to make the ones we have complete.

This is the exact process I go through every time I sit down to work on a book. It is not so much pulling aside to sit and write as it is a journey through ideas I have to mull over, figure out the connections between, and synthesize into a coherent presentation that will educate readers as well as keep you turning pages hungry for the next insight.

You don't know how often in that process, as I pray through my busy days and ask God to give me discernment, that I will come across a random book or run into someone I had never met who has just the key to understanding the next point I needed to make—or the crucial insight into stringing together a series of concepts I had been struggling with at that exact moment. It is not a clear, straightforward process, but I have to admit, it is exhilarating when all the words come together on the page. Until that time, it takes a good deal of determination and patience to see it through.

Despite its difficulties, this is the life to which I believe we are all called. There is no adventure—or growth for that matter—if there is no struggle. This is the life of purpose that gives our actions meaning. It is a life of being open, creative, and available to make a difference. And it is certainly not boring or monotonous. As we each walk out our calling, we can't afford to underestimate the importance of our individual parts in God's overall plan. Be we teachers, entrepreneurs, salespeople, parents, ministers, aid workers, construction specialists, pilots, senators, or whatever God has put into our hearts to be—we need to live from prospering, liberated souls grounded in spiritual priorities. We must nurture the innovative potentials within us by pressing forward, continuing to learn and grow, meditating in the spirit of prayer, and letting God speak through our accomplishments to the world.

God has empowered us with His Spirit, His Living Word, and with the power of prayer—and all the gifts of the Spirit, from the gift of prophecy to healing to words of knowledge.[11] We have the ability to tap into the wisdom of Heaven—not to mention the mind of Christ—in search of the answers and innovations the world needs.[12] "These inner technologies," writes author Gregg Braden, "represent our opportunity to first identify the future consequences of present-day choices, then to choose our future with confidence and trust."[13] Braden goes on to assert that it "is this inner science that empowers us to transcend with grace the challenges of life. In our collective wisdom lies the opportunity for a new era of peace, unity, and global cooperation unprecedented in human history."[14]

*Learn how to see. Realize that everything
connects to everything else.*

—LEONARDO DA VINCI

*The real art of discovery consists not in finding
new lands but in seeing with new eyes.*

—ALBERT SCHWEITZER

*The leaders in our culture are the people who see the
possibilities, who can go into a desert and see a garden.*

—ANTHONY ROBBINS, *UNLIMITED POWER*

History maker arise...and stir innovation breakthroughs.

Although there is "nothing new under the sun," there *are* new ways of combining and blending what is already here. Breakthroughs generally take time; ideas need to blend into innovation for discovery. When you diligently seek Creator God's guidance, He will use you as a world changer through the ideas, dreams, and visions He gives you.

Being aware of the spiritual intuition within you provides understanding regarding connections with others who have ideas that will complete the ones you have. Write all of the creative thoughts that come to mind in a notebook. Do not scoff at any idea that pricks your spirit—as it may be the one to set the world ablaze with environmental, social, or economic prosperity. Routinely speak to experts in the field, listen to podcasts, and read materials on the subjects that naturally intrigue you. Expanding your knowledge is always beneficial. Record all of your findings, then look for opportunities to mesh your ideas with others'—and enjoy the journey!

History maker arise...and pray for natural and supernatural connections.

Being open, creative, and available is certainly not a boring or monotonous life. Never underestimate the importance of your individual part in God's overall plan. Whatever God has put in your heart to be, you need to nurture the innovative potential within you by pressing forward, continuing to learn and grow, meditating in a spirit of prayer, and letting God speak through your accomplishments to the world.

Heavenly Father, I echo the author who wrote in the Book of Hebrews, "So let's do it—full of belief, confident that we're presentable inside and out. Let's keep a firm grip on the promises that keep us going. He always keeps His word. Let's see how inventive we can be in encouraging love and helping out."[15] *I pray that You will prepare me to receive all of the ideas, insights, and innovations You would have me contribute to the world for Your glory. Amen.*

CHAPTER TWELVE

how big is your world?

Security means the promotion of genuine possibility.
Real security is not about weapons. It's about the widest
possible range of people having enough faith about living
to see tomorrow—that they actually start to think about
the next day, the next week, the next year. It's about having
enough hope to plant in time for the spring season,
because you know that spring will come.

—SADAKO OGATA, FORMER UNITED NATIONS
HIGH COMMISSIONER FOR REFUGEES

So roll up your sleeves, put your mind in gear, be totally
ready to receive the gift that's coming.

—1 PETER 1:13 MSG

Facing continued unemployment and marginally effective social services, in 2004 the Netherlands passed the Work and Social Assistance Act to move toward decentralization, deregulation, and reduced administrative reporting. It essentially dismantled the structural hierarchy of the centralized government agency responsible for social security and welfare payments, putting the control of the local, chronically unemployed back into the hands of the people in those same communities. Part of the hope was that better service could be given to these local clients by local people who would have their hands and programs freed to more directly help their clients to reintegrate into the work force for the benefit of all.

In the municipality of Enschede, the consulting firm of Peer Facilitation was hired to work with those who had long been unemployed. They developed a course called "Upside Down" that the most able of the unemployed could attend. The consulting firm interviewed and selected candidates from the local area and invited them to a two-day workshop in which they would use Richard Barrett's Seven Levels of Consciousness Model and his Cultural Transformation Tools® (CTT) as means to evaluate and explore values and priorities, thoughts and feelings, needs and behaviors. The aim was to raise participants' mind-sets from level one awareness (survival) to an understanding of levels five and six consciousness (internal cohesion and making a difference).

Hopefully this would help them break the downward spiral of being long-term welfare recipients and inspire them to become self-sufficient once again. Formerly unemployed individuals who had gone through the workshops and made successful transitions off of welfare would serve as facilitators for the workshops. During the two days, participants would also be coached one on one, have an opportunity to meet with social services case workers, and come away with individualized plans for their futures. This would take place in four steps:

1. Selection and intake

2. Workshop participation

3. Values assessment

4. Follow-up

The average participant was 48 years old and had been unemployed about 11 years. Forty-five percent of them were non-Dutch, and 62 percent were women. The only requirement for participation was that they spoke Dutch. If they refused to participate, they faced losing their benefits, so there was motivation to at least get clients to the workshops. An average group consisted of 12 clients.

In a short video about the program sent to me by the Barrett Values Centre, it is easy to see that very few of the participants were eager to go or expected anything valuable out of the experience other than time away from their normal lives.[1] In the words of one woman interviewed on the video:

> I know all of this. They come with all of their plans of
> reintegration, etcetera. I have been busier with this [trying to
> reintegrate] than anything else. And now you are telling me
> you will change my life in two days.

Later she said she didn't see that it would do any good.

Another said:

> And now we will be locked up for two days. That seems like
> slavery to me…. Five years ago I asked for some help and
> nothing was available. Now I am forced to spend two days
> somewhere held in a room with a bunch of morons with whom
> I have nothing in common. I am going—otherwise my benefits
> will be cut. But I am not planning to participate in anything.
> No way!

Participants were bussed to a beautiful and serene location that was away from the city for the workshop. Peer leaders and case workers could then focus on the clients for a continuous period without interruption. This allowed the participants to feel valued and gave them time to change their focus and think in new patterns. It gave time for people to honestly connect with one another. The curriculum of the workshops included:

- Development of trust/having confidence in ourselves and others

- Recognizing and dealing with emotional intelligence

- Facing individual responsibility

- Discovery of passion

- Understanding of creativity

- Formulation of realistic goals

- Learning to coach one another

- Creating valuable relationships with others and ourselves

- Team building

- The development of our consciousness

- The creative cause: consciously choosing positive behavior

- The emotional layers of a human being: "from fear to leadership"

(Oddly enough, this is a list of ideas and concepts very much like what you have already read in this book!) The goal of day one was to shift from "I" to "we" thinking. Day two focused on finding meaning in society.

Despite their reluctance to participate, the two earlier interviewees had quite different things to say after the workshop began. As the first later said:

Quite a lot has happened to me, something that I did not expect in one and a half days. I didn't really believe it, yet something snapped. Leaving the past and the anger behind I can finally focus on the future, I hope. And I am happy to be here, in the present, with my two feet on the ground.

Others who participated in the same workshop said things like:

After these two days I have finally come to the conclusion that
I have been looking for excuses and blaming others. And now I
am more aware of my own emotions, which after all still exist.

And:

This morning I thought to myself it seems like we are
imprisoned by our own limitations. We talked about that
yesterday—that plate of armor—how we are trapped by our
own circumstances and our guilt towards others. They showed
us how to find the key to unlock our potential. The key lies
between stimulus and reaction.

The "Upside Down" program reverses the usual thinking about
behavior and outcomes. Rather than looking at behavior and analyzing
why people do what they do, it starts by identifying passions and then
how to choose the values and priorities that support that vision. Then it
looks at which emotions and thoughts contribute to realistic objectives
set according to the person's passion and purpose. Only after all of this
is done are behaviors looked at through the lens of choice. "How will I
act and what will I do knowing that this is my passion in life?"

Then a week after the workshops, individual follow-up coaching
sessions were scheduled to give participants feedback from their
personal values assessment surveys and to review their goals.

From March 2008 to June 2009, four out of ten of those participating
in the program became active members of society by finding jobs,
creating their own companies, volunteering, furthering their education,
or taking on an internship. During that time, unemployment benefits
were reduced, saving the local government over half a million dollars.
Not only that, but social workers who participated in the program were
re-energized by the process and began coming up with new ways of
structuring their work, reflecting on what they learned in the hope of
providing better services to their clients.[2]

Now, maybe you are thinking this is not an earth-shattering program because it is only in one small town in a remote place. But what if similar interactions were to take place in other communities around the world? What if the faith communities in our midst became centers of such innovative outreaches? How would it change attitudes? How would it reverse stereotypes? How would it shift paradigms—let alone the effects it has on people's industriousness, creativity, and renewed participation in their communities?

When individuals armed with the simple knowledge of developing the soul—of expanding consciousness—interact with others who are directionless and defeated, things change. Minds are renewed, hope is reborn, and purpose and passion take over lives. When people learn that they have the ability to choose differently and thus experience different results, they can't help but get excited about life. This starts a chain reaction of change—a revival of purpose—and lives take on new meaning.

It reminds me of the story of *The Wizard of Oz*. Dorothy came into a needy culture that lacked brains, heart, and courage in the Straw Man, the Tin Man, and the Cowardly Lion respectively. Together they embarked on a journey of discovery prompted by Dorothy's search for the place where she could be her authentic self. Strange things happen to businesses, churches, communities, and such when authentic people enter their midst. Authentic people have a way of helping us realize our own shortcomings while giving us hope to change. The change for the Straw Man, the Tin Man, and the Lion didn't come because Dorothy confronted them but because she lived out her authentic journey before them and with them. They decided to help her and, in the process, helped themselves.

Cultures only change when the individuals within them are touched in new ways, transforming mind-sets and attitudes. Authentic living defies groupthink and cannot be implemented *en masse*. This is why a great number of programs and training seminars fail; they don't reach into individual lives to give people heart, new mind-sets, or the courage to act on the behalf of others. This change only comes when the authentic person is injected into their lives—just like the counselors and workshop leaders of the "Upside Down" program. It was key that these leaders weren't from the ranks of the "successful," who more than likely would talk down to the unemployed, but were people who had emerged from the same population to which they were reaching out—and had their own powerful stories to tell. They were living, breathing examples of what healing your soul can look like.

One authentic person touches the life of another to inspire authenticity and actualization in them, and the chain reaction can be atomic in nature once it gets going. Until then, our businesses, houses of faith, organizations, and communities will just be houses of straw or empty containers afraid to reach toward their potential because they might fail. Until they see something different, they will be satisfied with the status quo—but when they meet authentic people maximizing their potential to fulfill their unique purpose, everything has a way of changing.

As human beings, we seek, above all things, to justify our existence—to have some vital means of making an impression of ourselves on the universe. We want to make some mark to show that we were here and that our having existed made some kind of difference to the humanity around us—even if that difference has only left a trail of tears and destruction. But we have a choice.

Those held captive by this world and its pain and suffering tend to propagate more of the same, but we can be delivered from that. We can choose to free our souls and act in love rather than out of fear. We can forever be trying to build our own Towers of Babel—monuments to ourselves—to reach our own interpretations of Heaven, to make a mark on the landscape of human history that will not only be remembered but make a lasting statement of who we were, even if that statement is a regrettable one—or, we can choose to flow in the same love that created the universe and is still creating good today. Sometimes our ambitions are not so grandiose, but the instinct is the same whether we are trying to build an empire or control every little thing anyone does who is within our realm of influence. It is the universal human struggle for significance and meaning.

If you have read this book to this point, I believe you are among those who desire to be the leaders of the future, who will take the high road of love rather than follow the low road of fear. You are not among those who will choose to define success only by what you can amass for yourself and those closest to you but will constantly look to see how you can be a blessing to others, even to those who oppose you. You will be a person with a worldview that is full of possibilities and who takes into account the needs of society and the environment as well as what it takes to make your company or organization prosperous. We have a choice to exploit or to edify, to corrupt or to set free. Whether we do it to an individual or a continent, we are ever either acting in our own interest or balancing "I" with the interests of "us." Selfishness is the root of all evil—the love of money is just one of the most blatant expressions of that selfishness. Once we realize the power of its influence, we have the ability to rise above it and choose the better way.

At the same time, we need to realize there have been some incredible creations that have emerged from selfish ambition and many acts of pure altruism that seem to have left little or no impression at all on the world. Empires have been built in the attempt to satisfy the soulish deficits of individual leaders. The world system, concerned only with physical manifestation, seldom recognizes anything but the outward appearance or the raw power of a business or government. We are moved by the flashy, not the true. We look at impact rather than depth of meaning and significance. The quick and dirty will always rival the longer road of diligence, patience, and empowerment. Having the emotional intelligence to do what is better for the long term rather than cashing in on the quick fixes of the present will always take discipline and training. We can no longer afford to get swept along with a system that exploits the future by offering short-term pleasures—that ultimately corrupts more than edifies. Too often, it takes us years to realize we have been fooled by a world system built on overconsumption and poor stewardship—one that will be self-destructive if we let it run its course uncorrected.

However, that is not what we were designed for. God had a different plan when He put each of us on the earth. He put us here to be stewards and fellow creators with Him. Never has the world more needed people to walk in that way—the Way, the Truth, and the Life—to become the shapers of history they were created to be.[3]

You see, the authentic you is exactly what the world needs most. Without it, quite frankly, we all suffer—and most especially those who haven't yet been born. What you choose to do with your life today—how you choose to invest it, the ripples of hope you create by the decisions you choose to make—will impact generations. You may not feel you owe it to yourself, or to the world, or that you or the world around you is worthy of it, but the future—a world of infinite possibilities we've not yet seen or imagined—is counting on you to tap into the infinite potential you carry.

With every approximation of the capacity we have to love, create, renovate, and restore, we suffer a little bit less, but we don't come anywhere near what is out there for us to achieve. When we become, in any one moment, exactly who we were created to be, it is as if everything in the universe aligns. When we are our authentic selves, it deals evil an irreparable, stunning blow, and grace is released into the atmosphere. Of course, such truly unselfish acts are rare, but their ramifications are immeasurable. Every dictator or tyrant who has ever lived is still fighting the good that was done in three years of ministry by Jesus of Nazareth. The humanity spread by Martin Luther King Jr., Mahatma Gandhi, and Nelson Mandela is still defeating racism.

Researchers and inventors are still defeating disease, poverty, and hunger with their innovations every day. One good person can alter his or her generation to the point that even enemies ultimately change for the better. The vision of an unshakably moral person transforms everything around that person to such a degree that it cannot be erased.

Nations crumble and rise, but what men and women such as these have released into the world goes on and on. The harder humankind has tried to destroy it, the more it spreads. The power of one authentic person at that person's creative best must never be underestimated— and our need for each other to become such people of change should never be neglected.

How does that speak to the role of the Church in these increasingly desperate times? It is a clarion call for the Church to rise up and take her rightful place—a Church comprised of individual members each being equipped to maximize his or her divine potential to shape history. The Church is not about buildings but about people—about you and I collectively bringing the power of God that is at work in each of us to affect change wherever it is we find ourselves in any given moment.[4]

No matter how dark the world becomes—how violent or oppressive, uncertain or chaotic, or unjust and ungodly—you and I as God's people can dispel that darkness. We know that in these last days the world will become darker, but we also know that even as it does, *"the earth will be filled with the knowledge of the glory of the Lord, as the waters cover the sea."*[5] In fact, as you see the darkness approaching, you can know for certain that this is your time to arise:

Arise, shine;
For your light has come!
And the glory of the Lord is risen upon you.
For behold, the darkness shall cover the earth,
And deep darkness the people;
But the Lord will arise over you,
And His glory will be seen upon you.[6]

The Church will be a voice in this end time, dictating the pace of things to the world. The world will continue to create problems and will look to God's people for solutions. We are called to be the light of the world, the salt of the earth—to have dominion and bring alignment into the arenas of industry, commerce, entertainment, banking, finance, innovation, education, governance, technology, and so much more.

Now it shall come to pass in the latter days
That the mountain of the Lord's house
Shall be established on the top of the mountains,
And shall be exalted above the hills;
And all nations shall flow to it.
Many people shall come and say,

"Come, and let us go up to the mountain of the Lord,
To the house of the God of Jacob;
He will teach us His ways,
And we shall walk in His paths."
For out of Zion shall go forth the law,
And the word of the Lord from Jerusalem.[7]

This is God's agenda for the Church. The Church is ordained for the top of the mountain—a place of governmental authority.[8] It's an exalted, prosperous place where we are able to meet the needs within our communities as well as bring solutions to global problems.[9] Our rightful place is at the top of the mountain, exalted above every situation—sitting in heavenly places and influencing the world as difference makers.[10] We are ambassadors of Christ, and no matter where we are, we will bring down the atmosphere of Heaven and establish Kingdom culture in whatever sphere of influence God has assigned us—where sickness gives way to healing, poverty gives way to prosperity, and doubt gives way to faith—until the Church's contract with the world and its communities has been fulfilled.[11]

The view is breathtaking. You don't have to endure the valley if you make the climb; either way it's the same energy. So choose the mountaintop. Put aside whatever is holding you back—*"lay aside every weight, and the sin which so easily ensnares us, and let us run with endurance the race that is set before us."*[12] Let's take our rightful place as the transformers of culture and history makers we have been put on earth to be.

Brothers and sisters, it is time to shape history!

I tell you the truth, anyone who believes in Me will do the
same works I have done, and even greater works.

—JOHN 14:12 NLT

The most important feature of Christ's character was...
His confidence in the greatness of the human soul.

—LEO TOLSTOY, *A CALENDAR OF WISDOM*

You are not here merely to make a living.
You are here in order to enable the world to live more
amply, with greater vision, with a finer spirit of hope and
achievement. You are here to enrich the world, and you
impoverish yourself if you forget the errand.

—WOODROW WILSON

History maker arise...and enlarge your world, your legacy!

Humans have struggled for significance and meaning since Cain murdered his brother Abel—the first two sons of Adam and Eve. People seek, above all things, to justify their existence, to make an impression on the universe—even if only with a bigger obituary headline than their neighbor's.

Actually shaping history, however, happens when one genuine and sincere person touches the life of another to inspire authenticity and actualization. A chain reaction can result exploding with positivity and multiplying exponentially. Until feeling the potency of your personal touch...businesses, churches, organizations, communities, your family and friends, will be afraid to reach toward their potential, fearing failure.

You can be the catalyst that leads to breaking through the status quo. Launch into a new venue, one where everyone you meet will see you as an authentic person maximizing your potential to fulfill your unique purpose. Attraction to you will be hard for others to resist—take them under your wing, mentor them, bring them along with you to right the wrongs, improve the circumstances, and expand the horizons near and far.

History maker arise...and pray for an awakened world.

Dear Lord, I fervently pray for divine wisdom to strike down disease and poverty with fierce, God-given intention. May I be one of the righteous people You use to change history for this generation and the next. Grant me the vision and the courage to take action in defense of the poor, wounded, and forgotten.

As nations battle for self-defined significance, Lord, raise up men and women who fight for Your glory on the frontlines in the spirit realm—where all battles begin—choosing to bring Heaven to earth so all can arise with dignity, enjoy equality, and embrace opportunity. Amen.

epilogue

FROM X FACTOR TO I FACTOR

I shall pass through this life but once. Any good, therefore,
that I can do, or any kindness I can show to any fellow
creature, let me do it now. Let me not defer or neglect
it for I shall not pass this way again.

—STEPHEN GRELLET

Watch what God does, and then you do it, like children who
learn proper behavior from their parents. Mostly what God
does is love you. Keep company with Him and learn a life of
love. Observe how Christ loved us. His love was not cautious
but extravagant. He didn't love in order to get something from
us but to give everything of Himself to us. Love like that.

—EPHESIANS 5:1–2 MSG

We started this book by asking the question, "What is wrong with
the world?" We did it looking for answers, looking for the solutions
that haven't been realized yet, what I would call the "X Factor." Like

solving an algebra equation, we want to find the value of "X"; we want to discover the unknown that will make sense of our lives and solve our problems. Somehow, internally, we know there must be an answer, and even if it is elusive, that answer is knowable.

I believe the answer to every problem is indeed knowable, for the answer to the X Factor is what I would call the "I Factor." Just as G. K. Chesterton inferred, if "I am" what's wrong with the world, "I am" also the answer to the problems that inundate it.

I'm not saying that there is one of us on this quest who will single-handedly solve all of the problems in the world, *but each of us living out our mission on the earth can make a world of difference* in the areas our thoughts and emotions return to again and again. There is a solution within each of us struggling to surface—we have to listen to that inner voice, educate our minds, discipline our souls, and courageously walk those answers out. As the old saying goes, "If it is to be, it's up to me." We must embrace the power of being our authentic selves—for that is the person in whom the answers we seek reside. They are not lurking somewhere outside of us, in some other sphere or organization or institution or program. They don't lie within some other person or collective people we anonymously call "them" but within *you* and *me*.

On the television show *The X Factor*, Simon Cowell and the other judges look for performers who have that intangible quality that will set them apart from the rest. They want to find the person who most exemplifies that "unknown special something" that will make them a star. I believe for each of us, there is a place where God has called us to be stars, but the element we need to get there is not an "X Factor" but the "I Factor." It is our identity, integrity, influence, and ability to innovate—each of us bringing our own piece of the puzzle, because the overall picture will never be complete without all of us participating.

As I travel around the world, people everywhere are on a quest toward authentic living—people are trying to find themselves; they are struggling to *be* themselves. They are seeking the freedom of fully realized selfhood—freedom to express themselves and become all that they are capable of becoming. *Authenticity* is a word that describes that quest. It is the process of *becoming*—becoming one's true self. It is a concept used to encapsulate all that is original and genuine and not an imitation of something else.

When Steve Jobs placed an "i" in front of his technological devices, he connected the individual person to technology, which not only spawned a new era for the Apple brand but for the entire world. His innovations created a new relationship between people and technology. His creations hit the world with such a force that they literally altered the way companies and individuals interacted with one another every time a new product or upgrade was announced. The "i" in the iPhone, iPod, iMac, iTouch, and iPad spoke to something that resonates in all of us—and that is the I Factor. Thumbing through his biographies, it became clear to me that he found his niche in this technological milieu by discovering his uniqueness as a gift to the world—and by unlocking the potential hidden within his distinctive perspective, he became an industry i-con (pun intended).

When Moses asked God His name at the burning bush, God replied simply, *"I Am."*[1] When you say, "I…" you connect yourself to the "I Am"—the Creator of Heaven and earth—the greatest innovator of all. When you utter the word "I," you fundamentally declare that you are an original—separate and distinct from every other creation of God. It is a declaration that you can know and be known distinct from everything and everyone else. The I Factor speaks to your originality, uniqueness, identity, and individuality. It speaks to the God-likeness with which you were created. If you can utter this one word, you have the power to live authentically.

Dare to maintain your originality. It is better to be uniquely you with all of your flaws and idiosyncratic behaviors than a perfect copy of someone else. Get to know your genuine self. Put time, energy, and resources into unlocking, discovering, nurturing, challenging, refining, grooming, and encouraging your greatest asset—the *you* God created for this place in *His*-story. Excavate the treasure hidden within. Take advantage of educational, social, and spiritual technologies that will cause your potential to flourish. When you don't know who you are, your potential is capped, your progress is hampered, and your success and prosperity are aborted. You become a product of your environment. You are forced to exist beneath glass ceilings, social barriers, psychological lids, and within stereotypes. But when you are empowered to discover your truest identity, glass ceilings are shattered, social barriers erased, psychological lids are removed, and stereotypes forgotten—you will see doors of opportunity swinging open for you; divine connections will appear as "chance meetings," and incredible networks will increase your worth and significance as you deliberately and consistently gain more and more skill in unearthing the gold mine of wealth hidden within your soul. The Spirit of God will lead you because you are a child of God.

The journey to authenticity is a progression. It begins with your own spiritual awakening—the divine being awakened within your spirit. Once the pilot light of your soul is lit, you can begin to understand who you were created to be. You will have eyes to see your true identity. In Latin this would be something like *saper vedere ego ipse*, or "knowing how to see one's true self." Once you have gained self-knowledge, you can develop the success skills needed to propel you toward significance—and once you understand how to expand your influence, you can begin to lead in the service of humanity. Your journey will bring you to your place of truth—a place where you tap into your potential—and in finding a platform for its expression you will make a lasting difference in this world.

Potential overlooked, unrealized, and underdeveloped is a threat to the advancement of humanity. By engaging in a capacity-building process, every single person can contribute to the health of their community and the prosperity of their nation. In today's globalized and rapidly changing societies, a single person's decision to embrace his or her potential for self-governance and leadership can create a wave of remarkable change. But in order to get there, emerging leaders often require guidance, resources, and support—hence the need for training practitioners in the discipline of Human Development Technologies (HDT).

Beginning with the assumption that every human being has the innate ability to contribute to the progress of humanity, HDT focuses on the pragmatic application of natural laws, socio-economic disciplines, principles of health and wellness, philosophies of education, psychotherapeutic empowerment strategies, and other capacity building processes that elevate the human condition and enhance lives.

The term "human development" became popularized in the 1990s as a result of widespread failure of efforts to boost the economies of chronically impoverished countries. At that time it was believed there was a close link between a country's economic growth and the degree of self-determination among its population—what Adam Smith referred to as the "invisible hand" of a free market economy. According to Mahbub ul Haq, founder of the Human Development Report:

> The basic purpose of development is to enlarge people's choices. In principle, these choices can be infinite and can change over time. People often value achievements that do not show up at all, or not immediately, in income or growth figures: greater access to knowledge, better nutrition and health services, more secure livelihoods, security against crime and physical violence, satisfying leisure hours, political and cultural freedoms and sense of participation in community activities. The objective of development is to create an enabling environment for people to enjoy long, healthy and creative lives.[2]

Harvard University professor and Nobel Laureate Amartya Sen stated, "Human development...is concerned with advancing the richness of human life, rather than the richness of the economy in which human beings live."[3]

The work of Mahbub ul Haq, Amartya Sen, and others has paved the way for a different approach to nation building—one that broadens the concept of human development by harnessing the dynamic power of being human in community. As humans, being in this world together, we are accountable to and for one another. We are each called to task when it comes to how we choose to live. We are duty bound to maximize our individual potential to create the greatest good for all.

Defined as the process of capacity building—enlarging people's choices and improving their capabilities—HDT asserts that no one need become a victim of circumstances or a product of their environment. When people are able to participate in decisions that affect their community, they are empowered to contribute to the overall progress, prosperity, and corporate destiny of their nation. This is the power of agency. "The true value of a human being," believed Albert Einstein, "is determined primarily by the measure and sense to which he has attained liberation."[4]

It is undeniable that people are the real wealth of nations and that no resource should be spared in providing the avenues, environments, and systems that will enable each person to maximize their creative potential. HDT, therefore, is about engaging individuals in the process of empowerment. It emphasizes capacity and character building, which act as the catalysts for sustainable change, continuous growth, and human advancement. Capacity building allows for the expansion of choices that people are able to make so they can live the life they value. When people are afforded opportunities to develop their decision-making capacity, they are able to build the character necessary to self-actualize. Character building underscores the importance of ethical and moral conduct in every aspect of our human dealings—whether on a personal, business, or civic level—and that is how nations prosper.

"As science continues to validate the relationship between our outer and inner worlds," wrote Gregg Braden in his now classic *The Isaiah Effect*, "it becomes more and more likely that a forgotten bridge links the world of our prayers with that of our experience."[5] I would add that it is becoming increasingly clear that a bridge links the world of our psychological, intellectual, and emotional state with that of our daily experiences, conditions, and realities. I agree with Braden's assertion that this link represents the best of all that science, philosophy, and religion have to offer—and that taken to new levels we will begin to conceive what we didn't understand was possible before.

It is upon these concepts of human development that I have built my Life Empowerment and Executive Coaching programs. My goal is to show you how to live authentically in order to lead authentically—to have the kind of confidence you need in yourself to be the kind of servant leader who transforms the world.[6] That is the purpose of this book and everything else I write—to empower you to transform yourself so you can transform the world around you. The other books in this series, beginning with *The 40 Day Soul Fast*, are all tools you can use to begin living more authentically. They will enable you to understand who you were created to be and why you are here. They will help you honor the divine within you that may very well be the light that dispels someone's darkness—the truth that not only sets you free but everyone with whom you come into contact.

Living authentically, in its simplest terms, is living from that truth—the truth in your heart and soul. It's allowing yourself to be guided by the divine and the wisdom made available to you by the Spirit of God each and every day. It is doing your best, most authentic, original work in the world. It's joyfully and deliberately living with dignity, meaning, and purpose and bringing that dignity and meaning to everyone around you—and by doing so, being your utmost for His Highest.

Authenticity is not always easy. It can be challenging and sometimes uncomfortable, but the rewards are worth the effort. It requires the courage and mental fortitude to say "no" to the pressure that comes from culture and to say "yes" to the transforming work of God welling up from within your heart.

Go and be that wellspring of life to someone else. Allow those "living waters" to flow forth from your own soul to a parched and thirsty world. As it says in Isaiah 58:10 (NKJV): *"Extend your soul to the hungry and satisfy the afflicted soul, then your light shall dawn in the darkness"*—or as it says in *The Message* version, *"Your lives will begin to glow in the dark."* You are the X Factor. *You* were created to be that shining star. You are destined to project light (wisdom, knowledge, insight; a revelation of Christ) into the dark places you encounter.

Read again the words of the song "Man in the Mirror," made famous by the late Michael Jackson. It sums up the message behind this book: "If you want to make the world a better place, take a look at yourself, and then make a change."

Change begins with the person you see in the mirror.

Don't sell yourself short and deprive this dark world of your own divine light. Your authentic, divine self is the seed of greatness God put on the inside of you the day He first thought of creating you—the deposit God made when He formed *"Christ in you, the hope of glory."*[7]

Embrace the glory God put within *you*. Cultivate it. Pursue it. Make it real.

And if you do, the world will never be the same again.

Your first job is to work on yourself. The greatest thing you can do for another human being is to get your own house in order and find your true spiritual heart.

—Ram Daas, *Polishing the Mirror*

We often confuse authority with power, but the two are not the same. Power works from the outside in, but authority works from the inside out.... Authority comes as I reclaim my identity and integrity, remembering my selfhood and my sense of vocation.

—Parker Palmer, *The Courage to Teach*

Change is an inside job.

—Shawn Stevenson

There's a place beyond right and wrong.
A place beyond the endless game of fixing what is seemingly broken.
Beyond all your best efforts to make this life work,
and to make your life's work matter.

It's here that you're faced
with the unfiltered voice
of your own soul.
A voice so unafraid
that it'll tell you of
your place in the world.
Of purpose and
unquestionable clarity.
And of your
belonging without condition.

It's here that personal revelation
can transform vulnerability
into vivid displays of
courage and strength.
In service to profound
connectedness and
a meaningful life.

—Nic Askew, "The Invitation" (nicaskew.com)

But the end is reconciliation; the end is redemption;
the end is the creation of the beloved community.
It is this type of spirit and this type of love that can
transform opponents into friends. It is this type of
understanding goodwill that will transform the deep
gloom of the old age into the exuberant gladness of the
new age. It is this love—the love of God, which will
bring about miracles in the hearts of men. This is the love
that may well be the salvation of our civilization.

—Martin Luther King Jr.

endnotes

INTRODUCTION

1. E. H. Lindley, "The New Frontier: Charge to the Class of 1932" (speech, the University of Nebraska, Lincoln, NE, June 4, 1932).

2. Ibid.

3. Napoleon Hill, *Think and Grow Rich* (Cleveland, OH: The Ralston Publishing Company, 1937), 27.

4. See Matthew 5–7; John 8:31–32; and John 13:31–35; Matthew 18:1–5; Mark 9:35, respectively.

5. See Acts 9:2; 19:9,23.

6. See Matthew 11:28–29 MSG.

7. See Galatians 5:25 NIV.

8. See Luke 17:21.

9. See Hebrews 6:19.

10. See Galatians 5:6.

11. See 2 Corinthians 5:14.

12. Robert F. Kennedy, "Day of Affirmation" (speech, University of Cape Town, South Africa, June 6, 1966), http://www.rfksafilm.org/html/speeches/unicape.php.

13. Hebrews 11:1 KJV, NLT.

14. "Whole," *The Free Dictionary*, http://www.thefreedictionary.com/wholeness.

15. "Wholeness," *The Merriam-Webster Dictionary* (Martinsburg, WV: Merriam-Webster, 2016).

16. Kennedy, "Day of Affirmation."

17. B. Drummond Ayres Jr., "Reagan Joins a Kennedy Remembrance," *NYTimes.com*, last modified June 6, 1981, http://www.nytimes.com/1981/06/06/us/reagan-joins-a-kennedy-remembrance.html.

18. See Colossians 1:27.

19. Matthew 12:21 NLT.

20. See John 14:27.

21. See Romans 14:17 and James 1:4, respectively.

CHAPTER ONE

1. *I Am*, directed by Tom Shadyac (2010; Boulder, CO: Gaiam, 2012), DVD.

2. Saad Abedine and Holly Yan, "Tunisian man sets himself on fire to protest unemployment," *CNN.com*, last modified March 12, 2013, http://www.cnn.com/2013/03/12/world/africa/tunisia -self-immolation/index.html.

3. Joe Sterling, "A year later, Bouazizi's legacy still burns," *CNN.com*, last modified December 17, 2011, http://www.cnn.com/2011/12/17/world/meast/arab-spring-one-year-later.

4. John 3:16–17.

5. "The Capacity to Dream: An Interview with Vincent Harding," *SGI Quarterly*, July 2014, http://www.sgiquarterly.org/feature2014jly-2.html.

6. Ibid.

7. 2 Peter 1:1 KJV. For reference to this call toward unity, see 1 Corinthians 1:10, Philippians 2:2, Romans 15:5, and Ephesians 4:3.

8. "About the Prize," *Templeton Prize*, http://www.templetonprize.org/abouttheprize.html; Paul Davies, "Physics and the Mind of God: The Templeton Prize Address" (speech, Templeton Prize Award Ceremony, London, England, May 3, 1995), http://cosmos.asu.edu/prize_ address.htm.

9. Richard Dawkins quoted in Gordon Fisher, *The Very Best of Richard Dawkins: Quotes from a Devout Atheist* (United States: Amazon Digital Services, 2015).

10. Matthew 6:10.

CHAPTER TWO

1. Darrow L. Miller, *Discipling Nations: The Power of Truth to Transform Cultures* (Seattle: YWAM Publishing, 1998), 38.

2. Ibid, 27.

3. Wangari Maathai, "What Do Trees Have to Do with Peace?" (speech, Nobel Lecture, Oslo, Norway, December 10, 1994), http://www.nobelprize.org/nobel_prizes/peace/laureates/2004/ maathai-lecture-text.html.

4. Visit www.cnnheroes.com to learn more.

5. James 2:18 NLT.

6. Titus 2:7 NKJV.

7. Romans 12:2 NKJV. See also See 2 Peter 1.

CHAPTER THREE

1. John S. Ferrell, *Fruits of Creation: A Look at Global Sustainability as Seen through the Eyes of George Washington Carver* (Shakopee, MN: Macalester Park Publishing, 1995), 50.

2. Ibid.

3. Matthew 10:8 NKJV.

4. "Quotes from George Washington Carver," *Carver Birthplace Association*, http://www .carverbirthplaceassoc.org/carver-quotes.

5. George Washington Carver quoted in Gary R. Kremer, ed., *George Washington Carver: In His Own Words* (Columbia, MO: The University of Missouri Press, 1987), 143.

6. See Ecclesiastes 3:11.

7. See Luke 8:10.

8. Genesis 1:3. See also Genesis 1:14–18.

9. James Strong, *The Exhaustive Concordance of the Bible: Showing Every Word of the Text of the Common English Version of the Canonical Books, and Every Occurrence of Each Word in Regular Order* (Ontario: Woodside Bible Fellowship, 1996), Hebrew #215 and #3874.

10. Genesis 1:15.

11. Proverbs 25:2 MSG.

12. Michelle Thaller, *The Universe: Light Speed*, dir. Darryl Rehr, History Channel, season 3, episode 3, 2008.

13. Einstein stated that the speed of light is the ultimate speed limit of the universe—nothing could travel faster than light. While this has long been held true, scientists are beginning to find things that do in fact travel faster than light. For example, galaxies at the end of the universe still expanding from the Big Bang are believed to still be traveling faster than light. However, space actually expands to match the speed of light, so that the distance travel is still technically the same. As far as we know, the only way to travel faster than this is in the spirit.

14. Genesis 1:2.

15. Genesis 1:3.

16. Isaiah 40:12.

17. Neil deGrasse Tyson, *The Universe: Beyond the Big Bang*, dir. Luke Ellis, History Channel, season 1, episode 14, 2007.

18. Robert Frost, "The Road Not Taken," in *The Road Not Taken: A Selection of Robert Frost's Poems*, ed. Louis Untermeyer (New York: Henry Holt, 1971), 270.

19. See Matthew 7:7.

20. Carver quoted in Kremer, ed., *George Washington Carver*, 143.

CHAPTER FOUR

1. Genesis 2:23.

2. John Donne, "Meditation XVII," *Literature Network*, http://www.online-literature.com/donne/ 409/.

3. 1 Thessalonians 5:23; emphasis added.

4. Mark 12:30; emphasis added.

5. Hebrews 4:12; emphasis added.

6. "Psychology." *Merriam-Webster's Collegiate Dictionary*, 10th ed. (United States: Merriam-Webster, 1998).

7. 1 Peter 3:4.

8. Christopher F. Monte, *Beneath the Mask: An Introduction to Theories of Personality* (New York: Holt, Rinehart and Winton, 1977), 129.

9. *Likesuccess.com*, http://likesuccess.com/1013517.

10. Ephesians 2:1–3.

11. Jeremiah 29:11.

12. John 10:10.

CHAPTER FIVE

1. The information and discussion in this chapter is taken largely from Curt Thompson's *The Anatomy of the Soul* (Carol Stream, IL: SaltRiver, 2010) and Caroline Leaf's *Who Switched Off My Brain?* (Nashville, TN: Thomas Nelson, 2009). These are wonderful resources that go into much more depth on this subject than I have room for here, and I highly recommend reading them.

2. See Genesis 2:20.

3. See Malcolm Gladwell, *Blink: The Power of Thinking without Thinking* (New York: Little, Brown, 2005).

4. See Philippians 4:7.

5. See Ephesians 6:11–12.

6. Mary Arsenault, "An Interview with Gregg Braden," *Wisdom Magazine*, http://wisdom-magazine.com/Article.aspx/563.

7. Matthew 7:5 NLT.

8. Michael Jackson, "Man in the Mirror," written by Siedah Garrett and Glen Ballard, http://play.google.com/music/preview/Tbmpeju6aio6w35hn7ovw3p2xby?lyrics.

CHAPTER SIX

1. Ephesians 5:14 NKJV.

2. Ecclesiastes 6:7–9 MSG.

3. Thompson, *Anatomy*, 44.

4. "70 Million Americans Feel Held Back by Their Past," *Barna Group*, last modified November 3, 2011, http://www.barna.org/culture-articles/532-70-million-americans-feel-held-back-by-their-past.

5. Ibid.

6. William Ernest Henley, "Invictus," *Poetry Foundation*, http://www.poetryfoundation.org/poems/51642/invictus.

7. Psalms 139:23–24 MSG.

8. Mark 12:30 NKJV; emphasis added.

9. Psalms 16:11 NIV.

CHAPTER SEVEN

1. As retold in Staci Boyer, *Motiva8n' U: 8 Core Tips That Will Give You the Strength to Lead a Healthy, Motiv8n' Lifestyle* (Aurora, IL: Medallion, 2010), 118–19.

2. Matthew 25:29 NKJV. For more on the "Matthew effect," see chapter 1 of Gladwell, *Outliers: The Story of Success* (New York: Little, Brown, 2008).

3. James 1:17 NKJV.

4. Proverbs 10:22.

5. Read my book *The Prosperous Soul: Your Journey to a Richer Life* (Shippensburg, PA: Destiny Image, 2015) for more on this topic.

6. See John 10:10.

7. Luke 16:10–12 NLT.

8. See John 6:5–13.

9. 1 Timothy 6:6 NKJV; emphasis added.

10. Philippians 4:11–13 NKJV.

11. E. G. Link, *Spiritual Thoughts on Material Things: Thirty Days of Food for Thought* (United States: Xulon, 2009), 97.

12. R. G. LeTourneau's autobiography, *Mover of Men and Mountains* (Chicago: Moody Publishers, 1960), is an excellent read for anyone interested in learning more about a world changer and understanding his mind-set, as well as just being a great story.

13. Shane Lopez, *Making Hope Happen: Create the Future You Want for Yourself and Others* (New York: Atria, 2013), 217.

14. Ibid.

15. Ibid.

16. Matthew 25:20–21 NKJV.

CHAPTER EIGHT

1. Jean M. Twenge, "The Age of Anxiety? Birth Cohort Change in Anxiety and Neuroticism, 1952–1993," *Journal of Personality and Social Psychiatry* 79, no. 6 (2000): 1007–21.

2. World Health Organization, *Health Behavior in School-Aged Children, 1996* (Calverton, MD: Macro International, 2001); S. Matthey and P. Petrovski, "The Children's Depression Inventory: Error in Cutoff Scores for Screening Purposes," *Psychological Assessment* 14, no. 2 (2002): 146–49.

3. Jo Anne Grunbaum et al., "Youth Risk Behavior Surveillance—United States, 2001," *Morbidity and Mortality Weekly Report* 51, no. SS-4 (2002), http://www.cdc.gov/mmwr/ preview/mmwrhtml/ss5104a1.htm.

4. S. A. Benton et al., "Changes in Counseling Center Client Problems across 13 Years," *Professional Psychology: Research and Practice* 34 , no. 1 (2003): 66–72.

5. J. Eccles and J. Appleton Gootman, eds., *Community Programs to Promote Youth Development* (Washington, DC: National Academies P, 2002).

6. The Commission on Children at Risk, *Hardwired to Connect: The New Scientific Case for Authoritative Communities* (New York: The Institute for American Values, 2003), 9.

7. Ibid., 14.

8. "40 Developmental Assets for Adolescents," *Search Institute*, http://www.search-institute .org/content/40-developmental-assets-adolescents-ages-12-18.

9. See 1 John 4:8.

10. Proverbs 11:30 NKJV.

11. Stephen R. Covey, *Principle-Centered Leadership* (New York: Free Press, 2003), 287.

12. Luke 1:37.

13. Luke 4:18–19 NKJV.

14. James 5:16 NIV.

15. See Hebrews 5:7 NIV.

16. See my prayer companion *Atomic Power of Prayer* (Compact Disc, Trimm International, 2016).

CHAPTER NINE

1. 1 Corinthians 12:31.

2. 1 John 1:9; James 5:16.

3. Ephesians 4:15–16.

4. Mark 12:30; Mark 12:31; emphasis added.

5. "The Barrett Model," *Barrett Values Centre*, http://www.valuescentre.com/mapping-values/ barrett-model.

6. Barrett leadership training is available online at http://tnlp.valuescentre.com.

7. See http://www.savoryinstitute.com for more information.

8. See the section on "Social Prosperity" in *The Prosperous Soul*.

CHAPTER TEN

1. See Ecclesiastes 9:13–16.

2. Shoshana Zuboff, "The Old Solutions Have Become New Problems," *Bloomberg Business-week*, last modified July 2, 2009, http://www.businessweek.com/managing/content/jul2009/ca2009072_489734.htm.

3. Michael Jacobs, "How Business Schools Have Failed Business," *Wall Street Journal*, last modified April 24, 2009, http://online.wsj.com/article/SB124052874488350333.html.

4. Rosabeth Moss Kanter, "Ten Essentials for Getting Value from Values," *Harvard Business Review*, last modified June 14, 2010, http://blogs.hbr.org/kanter/2010/06/ten-essentials-for-getting-val.html.

5. 1 Corinthians 12:14–19.

6. Kanter, "Adding Values to Valuations: Indra Nooyi and Others as Institution-Builders," *Harvard Business Review*, last modified May 3, 2010, http://blogs.hbr.org/imagining-the-future-of-leadership/2010/05/adding-values-to-valuations-in.html.

7. Tex Gunning, "I Have No Choice: An Interview with Tex Gunning," *EnlightenNext Magazine* 28 (March–May 2005): 96.

8. Richard Barrett, *The New Leadership Paradigm* (Asheville, NC: Barrett Values Centre, 2010).

9. Ibid., 21.

10. Ibid.

11. Ralph Waldo Emerson, quoted in Patrick Daniel, "Self-Reliance: An Introduction to Ralph Waldo Emerson," *Medium*, last modified May 13, 2014, http://medium.com/patrickdaniel/self-reliance-an-introduction-to-ralph-waldo-emerson-4fa4424a6eda.

12. Emerson, quoted in John C. Maxwell, *Put Your Dream to the Test: 10 Questions That Will Help You See It and Seize It* (Nashville, TN: Thomas Nelson, 2011), 148.

CHAPTER ELEVEN

1. Genesis 11:6.

2. Read *The 40 Day Soul Fast: Your Journey to Authentic Living* (Shippensburg, PA: Destiny Image, 2011) and *Reclaim Your Soul: Your Journey to Personal Empowerment* (Shippensburg, PA: Destiny Image, 2014). for practical guidance.

3. Proverbs 25:2.

4. Ecclesiastes 1:9.

5. Steven Johnson, *Where Good Ideas Come From: The Natural History of Innovation* (New York: Riverhead Books, 2010), 151–53.

6. Michael Michalko, *Creative Thinkering: Putting Your Imagination to Work* (Novato, CA: New World Library, 2011), 54.

7. Leonard Cohen, "Anthem," *The Future*, Compact Disc, Columbia Records, 1992.

8.   Michalko, *Creative Thinking*, xvii.

9.   Ken Williams quoted in Johnson, *Where Good Ideas Come From*, 69.

10.   Johnson, *Where Good Ideas Come From*, 153.

11.   See 1 Corinthians 12:8–10.

12.   See 1 Corinthians 2:16.

13.   Gregg Braden, *The Isaiah Effect: Decoding the Lost Science of Prayer and Prophecy* (New York: Three Rivers Press, 2000), 50.

14.   Ibid., 23.

15.   Hebrews 10:24–25 MSG.

CHAPTER TWELVE

1.   "OndersteBoven [Upside Down]," Municipality Enschede and Management Consulting Firm Peer Facilitation, TV Enschede FM.

2.   For more on the "Upside Down" program, see Richard Barrett's blog at http://richardbarrett .posterous.com/working-with-consciousness-and-values-in-comm.

3.   See John 14:6.

4.   See Ephesians 3:20.

5.   Habakkuk 2:14.

6.   Isaiah 60:1–2 NKJV.

7.   Isaiah 2:2–3 NKJV.

8.   See Isaiah 9:6–7.

9.   See Deuteronomy 28:1–14; Ephesians 3:10–11.

10.   See Ephesians 2:6.

11.   See 2 Corinthians 5:20; Matthew 24:14; Mark 16:15–18.

12.   Hebrews 12:1 NKJV.

EPILOGUE

1.   Exodus 3:14.

2.   "About Human Development," *Human Development Reports*, United Nations Development Program, http://hdr.undp.org/en/humandev.

3.   Ibid.

4.   Albert Einstein, *The World as I See It* (London: The Bodley Head Limited, 1935), 7.

5. Braden, *The Isaiah Effect*, xviii.

6. To learn how you can incorporate these principles into your daily life, please visit www .trimmcoaching.com.

7. Colossians 1:27.

The list of 40 Developmental Assets® is used with permission from Search Institute®. Copyright © 1997, 2006 Search Institute, Minneapolis, MN 55413; www.search-institute.org.

bibliography

"40 Developmental Assets for Adolescents." *Search Institute*. http://www.search-institute.org/content/40-developmental-assets-adolescents-ages-12-18.

"70 Million Americans Feel Held Back by Their Past." *Barna Group*. Last modified November 3, 2011. http://www.barna.org/culture-articles/532-70-million-americans-feel-held-back-by-their-past.

Abedine, Saad, and Holly Yan. "Tunisian man sets himself on fire to protest unemployment." *CNN.com*. Last modified March 12, 2013. http://www.cnn.com/2013/03/12/world/africa/tunisia-self-immolation/index.html.

"About Human Development." *Human Development Reports*. United Nations Development Program. http://hdr.undp.org/en/humandev.

"About the Prize." *Templeton Prize*. http://www.templetonprize.org/abouttheprize.html.

Arsenault, Mary. "An Interview with Gregg Braden." *Wisdom Magazine*. http://wisdom-magazine.com/Article.aspx/563.

Askew, Nic. "The Invitation." *Nicaskew.com*. http://nicaskew.com/blog/truth-freedom-and-an-invitation/.

Ayres Jr., B. Drummond. "Reagan Joins a Kennedy Remembrance." *NYTimes.com*. Last modified June 6, 1981. http://www.nytimes.com/1981/06/06/us/reagan-joins-a-kennedy-remembrance.html.

Barrett, Richard. *The New Leadership Paradigm*. Asheville, NC: Barrett Values Centre, 2010.

"The Barrett Model." *Barrett Values Centre*. http://www.valuescentre.com/mapping-values/barrett-model.

225

Benton, S. A., et al. "Changes in Counseling Center Client Problems across 13 Years." *Professional Psychology: Research and Practice* 34 , no. 1 (2003): 66–72.

Berry, Wendell. "Sex, Economy, Freedom, and Community." In *Sex, Economy, Freedom & Community: Eight Essays*, 117–74. New York: Pantheon, 1993.

———. *The Unsettling of America: Culture & Agriculture*. San Francisco, CA: Sierra Club Books, 1977.

Bogunovic, Dragan P. *Heavenly Wisdom: Talent, Imagination, Creativity and Wisdom*. Bloomington, IN: AuthorHouse, 2013.

Boyer, Staci. *Motiva8n' U: 8 Core Tips That Will Give You the Strength to Lead a Healthy, Motiv8n' Lifestyle*. Aurora, IL: Medallion, 2010.

Braden, Gregg. *The Isaiah Effect: Decoding the Lost Science of Prayer and Prophecy*. New York: Three Rivers Press, 2000.

Buscaglia, Leo. *Love: What Life Is All About...*. New York: Fawcett Columbine, 1972.

Call the Midwife. Directed by Lisa Clarke. PBS, season 5, episode 6, 2016.

"The Capacity to Dream: An Interview with Vincent Harding." *SGI Quarterly*, July 2014. http://www.sgiquarterly.org/feature2014jly-2.html.

Chopra, Deepak, and Oprah Winfrey. *Creating Peace from the Inside Out: The Power of Connection*. Compact Disc. The Chopra Center, B01M6ZKN6T. 2016.

Cohen, Leonard. "Anthem." *The Future*. Compact Disc. Columbia Records. 1992.

The Commission on Children at Risk. *Hardwired to Connect: The New Scientific Case for Authoritative Communities*. New York: The Institute for American Values, 2003.

Covey, Stephen R. *Principle-Centered Leadership*. New York: Free Press, 2003.

Daas, Ram. *Polishing the Mirror: How to Live from Your Spiritual Heart*. Boulder, CO: Sounds True, 2013.

Daniel, Patrick. "Self-Reliance: An Introduction to Ralph Waldo Emerson." *Medium*. Last modified May 13, 2014. http://medium.com/patrickdaniel/self-reliance-an-introduction-to-ralph-waldo-emerson-4fa4424a6eda.

Davies, Paul. "Physics and the Mind of God: The Templeton Prize Address." Templeton Prize Award Ceremony, London, England, May 3, 1995. http://cosmos.asu.edu/prize_address.htm.

Donne, John. "Meditation XVII." *Literature Network*. http://www.online-literature.com/donne/409/.

Eccles, J., and J. Appleton Gootman, eds. *Community Programs to Promote Youth Development.* Washington, DC: National Academies Press, 2002.

Einstein, Albert. *The World as I See It.* London: The Bodley Head Limited, 1935.

Ferrell, John S. *Fruits of Creation: A Look at Global Sustainability as Seen through the Eyes of George Washington Carver.* Shakopee, MN: Macalester Park Publishing, 1995.

Fisher, Gordon. *The Very Best of Richard Dawkins: Quotes from a Devout Atheist.* United States: Amazon Digital Services, 2015.

Ford, Martin Eugene. *Motivating Humans: Goals, Emotions, and Personal Agency Beliefs.* Newbury Park, CA: SAGE, 1992.

Frost, Robert. "The Road Not Taken." In *The Road Not Taken: A Selection of Robert Frost's Poems,* edited by Louis Untermeyer. New York: Henry Holt, 1971.

Gladwell, Malcolm. *Blink: The Power of Thinking without Thinking.* New York: Little, Brown, 2005.

———. *Outliers: The Story of Success.* New York: Little, Brown, 2008.

Goleman, Daniel. *Social Intelligence: The New Science of Human Relationships.* New York: Bantam, 2006.

Goodlet, Carlton Benjamin. *Sun-Reporter* (San Francisco, CA).

Grellet, Stephen. In "Life," vs. 1–3. *Hoyt's New Cyclopedia of Practical Quotations.* New York: Funk & Wagnalls, 1922. http://www.bartleby.com/78/476.html.

Grunbaum, Jo Anne, et al. "Youth Risk Behavior Surveillance—United States, 2001." *Morbidity and Mortality Weekly Report* 51, no. SS-4 (2002). http://www.cdc.gov/mmwr/preview/mmwr html/ss5104a1.htm.

Gunning, Tex. "I Have No Choice: An Interview with Tex Gunning." *EnlightenNext Magazine,* 28 (March–May 2005): 95–98.

Hale, Edward Everett. "I Am Only One." *Bartlett's Familiar Quotations,* compiled by John Bartlett, 4th ed., 717. Boston: Little, Brown, 1968.

Hecshel, Abraham Joshua. "The Reasons for My Involvement in the Peace Movement." In *Moral Grandeur and Spiritual Audacity,* edited by Susannah Heschel, 224–26. New York: Farrar, Straus and Giroux, 1996.

———. *Who Is Man?* Stanford, CA: Stanford University Press, 1965.

Henley, William Ernest. "Invictus," *Poetry Foundation,* http://www.poetryfoundation.org/poems/51642/invictus.

Hill, Napoleon. *Think and Grow Rich.* Cleveland, OH: The Ralston Publishing Company, 1937.

I Am. Directed by Tom Shadyac. 2010. Boulder, CO: Gaiam, 2012. DVD.

Jackson, Michael. "Man in the Mirror." Written by Siedah Garrett and Glen Ballard. *Google Play*. http://play.google.com/music/preview/Tbmpeju6aio6w35hn7ovw3p2xby?lyrics.

Jacobs, Michael. "How Business Schools Have Failed Business." *Wall Street Journal*. Last modified April 24, 2009. http://online.wsj.com/article/SB124052874488350333.html.

Johnson, Steven. *Where Good Ideas Come From: The Natural History of Innovation*. New York: Riverhead Books, 2010.

Kanter, Rosabeth Moss. "Adding Values to Valuations: Indra Nooyi and Others as Institution-Builders." *Harvard Business Review*. Last modified May 3, 2010. http://blogs.hbr.org/imagining-the-future-of-leadership/2010/05/adding-values-to-valuations-in.html.

———. "Ten Essentials for Getting Value from Values." *Harvard Business Review*. Last modified June 14, 2010. http://blogs.hbr.org/kanter/2010/06/ten-essentials-for-getting-val.html.

Kennedy, Robert F. "Day of Affirmation." University of Cape Town, South Africa, June 6, 1966. http://www.rfksafilm.org/html/speeches/unicape.php.

———. *Robert Kennedy, in His Own Words*, edited by Edwin O. Guthman and Jeffrey Shulman. New York: Bantam, 1988.

Kierkegaard, Søren. *Either / Or: A Fragment of a Life*. London: Penguin, 1992.

King Jr., Martin Luther. "Nonviolence: The Only Road to Freedom." *Ebony Magazine* (1966): 27–30, 32, 34. http://www.thekingcenter.org/archive/document/nonviolence-only-road-freedom.

Kremer, Gary R., ed. *George Washington Carver: In His Own Words*. Columbia, MO: The University of Missouri Press, 1987.

Leaf, Caroline. *Who Switched Off My Brain?* Nashville, TN: Thomas Nelson, 2009.

LeTourneau, R. G. *Mover of Men and Mountains*. Chicago: Moody Publishers, 1960.

Likesuccess.com. http://likesuccess.com/1013517.

Lindley, E. H. "The New Frontier: Charge to the Class of 1932." Commencement speech delivered the University of Nebraska, Lincoln, NE, June 4, 1932.

Link, E. G. *Spiritual Thoughts on Material Things: Thirty Days of Food for Thought*. United States: Xulon, 2009.

Lopez, Shane. *Making Hope Happen: Create the Future You Want for Yourself and Others*. New York: Atria, 2013.

Maathai, Wangari. "What Do Trees Have to Do with Peace?" Nobel Lecture, Oslo, Norway, December 10, 1994. http://www.nobelprize.org/nobel_prizes/peace/laureates/2004/maathai-lecture-text.html.

MacMillan, Amy. "Know Your Own Beliefs." *News @ MITSloan* 18, no. 6 (March 9, 2009), 5–6. PDF.

Matthey, S., and P. Petrovski, "The Children's Depression Inventory: Error in Cutoff Scores for Screening Purposes." *Psychological Assessment* 14, no. 2 (2002): 146–49.

Maxwell, John C. *Put Your Dream to the Test: 10 Questions That Will Help You See It and Seize It*. Nashville, TN: Thomas Nelson, 2011.

Michalko, Michael. *Creative Thinkering: Putting Your Imagination to Work*. Novato, CA: New World Library, 2011.

Miller, Darrow L. *Discipling Nations: The Power of Truth to Transform Cultures*. Seattle, WA: YWAM, 1998.

Mindwalk. Directed by Bernt Amadeus Capra. 1991. Hollywood, CA: Paramount, 1998. VHS.

Monte, Christopher F. *Beneath the Mask: An Introduction to Theories of Personality*. New York: Holt, Rinehart and Winton, 1977.

Ogata, Sadako. "Security Check." Interviewed by Christine Canabou. *Fast Company*. May 31, 2001. http://www.fastcompany.com/44899/security-check.

"OndersteBoven [Upside Down]," Municipality Enschede and Management Consulting Firm Peer Facilitation, TV Enschede FM.

Palmer, Parker. *The Courage to Teach: Exploring the Inner Landscape of a Teacher's Life*. San Francisco, CA: Jossey-Bass, 2007.

———. *Healing the Heart of Democracy: The Courage to Create a Politics Worthy of the Human Spirit*. San Francisco, CA: Jossey-Bass, 2011.

———. *A Hidden Wholeness: The Journey Toward an Undivided Life*. San Francisco, CA: Jossey-Bass, 2004.

———. *Let Your Life Speak: Listening for the Voice of Vocation*. San Francisco, CA: Jossey-Bass, 2000.

"Psychology." *Merriam-Webster's Collegiate Dictionary*. 10th ed. United States: Merriam-Webster, 1998.

Ritterman, Jeff. "The Beloved Community: Martin Luther King Jr.'s Prescription for a Healthy Society." *Huffington Post*. Last modified March 21, 2014. http://www.huffingtonpost.com/jeffrey-ritterman/the-beloved-community-dr-_b_4583249.html.

Robbins, Anthony. *Unlimited Power: The New Science of Personal Achievement*. New York: Free Press, 1986.

Rudan, Gina. *Five Steps to Practical Genius*. Podcast. *BTalk*. BNET Australia, 2012, http://www.mixcloud.com/bnetaustralia-bnetaustraliapod/five-steps-to-practical-genius-btalk/.

"Shane Lopez: Hope Is an Ancient Virtue." *Faith & Leadership*. Last modified April 21, 2014. http://www.faithandleadership.com/qa/shane-lopez-hope-ancient-virtue.

Shepherd, Philip. *New Self, New World: Recovering Our Senses in the Twenty-First Century*. Berkeley, CA: North Atlantic Books, 2010.

Sterling, Joe. "A year later, Bouazizi's legacy still burns." *CNN.com*. Last modified December 17, 2011. http://www.cnn.com/2011/12/17/world/meast/arab-spring-one-year-later.

Strong, James. *The Exhaustive Concordance of the Bible: Showing Every Word of the Text of the Common English Version of the Canonical Books, and Every Occurrence of Each Word in Regular Order*. Ontario: Woodside Bible Fellowship, 1996.

Thaller, Michelle. *The Universe: Light Speed*. Written and directed by Darryl Rehr. *History Channel*, season 3, episode 3, 2008.

Thompson, Curt. *The Anatomy of the Soul*. Carol Stream, IL: SaltRiver, 2010.

Tolstoy, Leo. *A Calendar of Wisdom*. New York: Scribner, 1997.

Trimm, Cindy. *The 40 Day Soul Fast: Your Journey to Authentic Living*. Shippensburg, PA: Destiny Image, 2011.

———. *Atomic Power of Prayer*. Compact Disc. Trimm International, 2016.

———. *The Prosperous Soul: Your Journey to a Richer Life*. Shippensburg, PA: Destiny Image, 2015.

———. *Reclaim Your Soul: Your Journey to Personal Empowerment*. Shippensburg, PA: Destiny Image, 2014.

Twenge, Jean M. "The Age of Anxiety? Birth Cohort Change in Anxiety and Neuroticism, 1952–1993." *Journal of Personality and Social Psychiatry* 79, no. 6 (2000): 1007–21.

Tyson, Neil deGrasse. *The Universe: Beyond the Big Bang*. Written by Matt Hickey and directed by Luke Ellis. History Channel, season 1, episode 14, 2007.

Welty, Eudora. *One Time, One Place: Mississippi in the Depression*. Rev. ed. Jackson, MS: University of Mississippi Press, 1996.

"Whole." *The Free Dictionary*. http://www.thefreedictionary.com/wholeness.

"Wholeness." *The Merriam-Webster Dictionary*. Martinsburg, WV: Merriam-Webster, 2016.

Wiesel, Elie. Interview in *U.S. News & World Report*. October 27, 1986.

———. Nobel Lecture, Oslo, Norway, December 10, 1985, http://www.nobelprize.org/nobel_prizes/peace/laureates/1986/wiesel-acceptance_en.html.

Wilkerson, Isabel. "The Heart Is the Last Frontier." By Krista Tippett. *On Being with Krista Tippett* (November 17, 2016). http://onbeing.org/programs/isabel-wilkerson-the-heart-is-the-last-frontier/.

Williams Terry Tempest. "Engagement," *Orion Magazine.* http://orionmagazine.org/article/engagement/.

Wilson, Woodrow. "Address of President Woodrow Wilson, Delivered at Swarthmore College." An address delivered at Swarthmore College, Swarthmore, PA, October 25, 1913. http://archive.org/stream/addressofpreside07wilsonw.

World Health Organization, *Health Behavior in School-Aged Children, 1996.* Calverton, MD: Macro International, 2001.

Zuboff, Shoshana. "The Old Solutions Have Become New Problems." *Bloomberg Businessweek.* Last modified July 2, 2009. http://www.businessweek.com/managing/content/jul2009/ca2009072_489734.htm.

About Dr. Cindy Trimm

As a best-selling author, keynote speaker, and former senator of Bermuda, Dr. Trimm is a sought-after empowerment specialist, thought leader, and advocate for cultural change. Listed among *Ebony* magazine's *Power 100* as the "top 100 doers and influencers in the world today," Dr. Trimm consults with civic, nonprofit, and religious leaders around the world. With a background in government, education, psychology, and human development, Dr. Trimm translates powerful spiritual truth into everyday language that empowers individuals to transform their lives and their communities.

Trimm International is a pioneering force in the personal and leadership development field. On the forefront of transforming culture through empowering individuals to lead change, Trimm International provides cutting-edge programs and innovative products that inspire, equip, and empower people to impact their world.

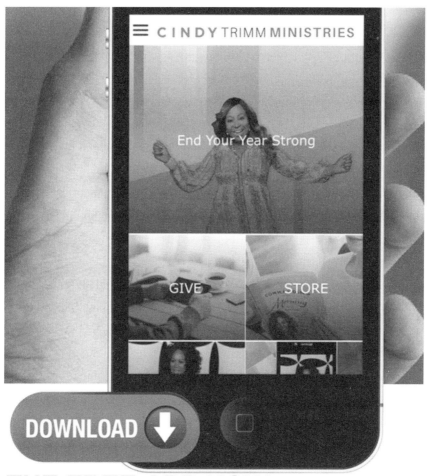

THE FREE APP NOW

KINGDOM™
SCHOOL OF MINISTRY

FREE E-BOOKS?
YES, PLEASE!

Get **FREE** and deeply discounted **Christian books** for your **e-reader** delivered to your inbox **every week!**

IT'S SIMPLE!

VISIT lovetoreadclub.com

SUBSCRIBE by entering your email address

RECEIVE free and discounted e-book offers and inspiring articles delivered to your inbox every week!

Unsubscribe at any time.

SUBSCRIBE NOW!

LOVE TO READ CLUB

visit **LOVETOREADCLUB.COM** ▶